A Season to Remem

COLCHESTER UNITED
1991/92

GM Vauxhall Conference Champions (right)
and Vauxhall FA Trophy winners, 1991/92.

A Season to Remember

COLCHESTER UNITED
1991/92

JEFF WHITEHEAD & MATT HUDSON

TEMPUS

ACKNOWLEDGEMENTS

We would like to record our thanks to Scott Dolling at the *East Anglian Daily Times* for his valued support for this book, to his colleagues Sharon Boswell and Liz Rozier; Jerry Carter of Colchester United and Michael J Middleton.

Thanks is also due to *East Anglian Daily Times* journalists Neal Manning and Elvin King and the wonderful images captured by staff photographers Owen Hines, Nicky Lewin and John Kerr. Similarly to Tony Williams (www.thenon-leaguepaper.com) and the *FA Non-League Directory* and its staff photographers of 1991/92: Gavin Ellis, John Robinson, Dave West, Rob Ruddock, Paul Dennis and Duncan Cook. Finally to Marilyn Whitehead, just because.

Every effort has been made to acknowledge the original source of copyright for all the pictures in this book.

Page 1: The FA Trophy (left) and the GM Vauxhall Conference Championship Trophy.

Frontispiece: Every fans dream: The championship, his clubs first-ever trip to Wembley Stadium, a double-clinching victory at the home of legends and a swift return to the Football League.

First published 2002

Tempus Publishing Limited
The Mill, Brimscombe Port,
Stroud, Gloucestershire, GL5 2QG

© Jeff Whitehead and Matt Hudson 2002

The right of Jeff Whitehead and Matt Hudson to be identified as the Authors of this work has been asserted by them in accordance with the Copyrights, Designs and Patents Act 1988.

British Library Cataloguing in Publication Data.
A catalogue record for this book is available from the British Library.

ISBN 0 7524 2712 1

Typesetting and origination by Tempus Publishing Limited
Printed in Great Britain by Midway Colour Print, Wiltshire

Foreword

Roy McDonough (Player-Manager)

When previous player-manager Ian Atkins departed for Birmingham at the eleventh hour, I found myself in the right place at the right time. I had always wanted to become a manager one day, but found myself at the relatively tender age of thirty-three in charge of a team with no budget and the unenviable task of hauling the club back into the Football League. Having failed to achieve that goal the previous season, the club was at a crossroads and failure this time could have spelt the end for Colchester United.

My players thrived on team spirit and one of my main motivations was the many 'doubters' who insisted that I was not up to the task. I feel that we took Conference football in our stride, and personally I recorded my best ever seasonal goal tally. It was certainly a very proud moment to lead the boys out at Wembley just days after taking the Conference crown. We won the duel with Wycombe fair and square, we beat them twice, even toyed with them at Layer Road when 3-0 up, and finished worthy Champions. There is no denying that they had the better set-up and were a bigger and stronger side than us, but boy could they whinge!

I've no doubt that if I would have been able to keep that squad together and been given some funds to strengthen it, then we would have made it to Division Two much earlier than the club actually did. My only regret is that I never got the chance to manage from the sidelines for any length of time, as I felt that my influence and experience was in greater need on the pitch.

I am delighted that this particular season has been chosen as Colchester United's 'Most Memorable' against stiff opposition from the 1948 and 1971 FA Cup campaigns. I am sure fans will enjoy reliving what was truly a remarkable chapter in both my own professional career and indeed the club's history.

Tony English (Captain).

When I was asked to contribute a foreword for this book, it really didn't seem possible that it was ten years ago that we managed to achieve the famous non-League double. They really were amazing days, and having kept together the squad that Ian Atkins had assembled, Roy McDonough did a great job to get us promoted that year.

As a boy, I had always dreamed of being captain and lifting either a championship or a cup. And here I was doing both in the same season. It was something I'll never forget and the memories will live on. The support that day was brilliant, as it had been all season. Wherever we went, we had as many as 2,000 supporters following us and I still vividly recall the fantastic backing for virtually every game home and away that year.

I remember the rivalry with Wycombe that season as we both fought for the title. Who can forget the fact that goalkeeper Scott Barrett scored that goal with a kick from his own area at Adams Park? When you look back at the league table and see that we only went up on goal difference, there couldn't have been many more important goals scored that year.

The size of our achievement took some time to sink in. To be honest, it wasn't until the pre-season campaign for the next season that it really dawned on us all. I remember we faced Norwich City here at Layer Road, and I came face to face with Ian Butterworth.

Ian and I had been schoolboys together at Coventry City, and whilst I had come down to Colchester, he had spent most of his career in the top two divisions with Norwich. So when he told me that he had not even come close to playing at the famous Twin Towers, it made me realise what we had actually accomplished.

Whilst ten years have flown past, it is a great credit to the club that they find themselves in the position they do today. Colchester United are now an established Division Two side and for a club of our size and finances, it is a fantastic achievement that everyone should be proud of.

Mark Kinsella (Midfielder and since World Cup 2002 Republic of Ireland International)

I had watched the FA Cup finals as a lad back in Ireland and it was a dream of mine to play at Wembley. Having watched those games on TV, little could I have known that after leaving home for Colchester at the tender age of fifteen that I would be playing at that famous stadium just over three years later.

The Wycombe Wanderers game was an important one for us that season, and those three points proved vital. But I think the fixture that made us believe we could go on and win the Conference was the game against Macclesfield at Moss Rose. We were leading 2-1 but then fell 4-2 behind, and it was only two goals from Tony English that hauled us back to four apiece. That game typified the team spirit we had and the qualities that we possessed throughout that season.

The key was our brilliant strikeforce. With Steve McGavin, Gary Bennett and Roy

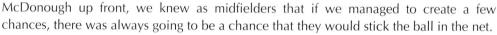

McDonough up front, we knew as midfielders that if we managed to create a few chances, there was always going to be a chance that they would stick the ball in the net.

Roy was a typical player manager, and did things very much his own way. He always stuck by his players and that meant that the players were always working for him. I also have to say a good word for Steve Foley who looked after me when I arrived from Ireland. I feel sure that had Steve not treated me so well when I first came to Colchester United, then the homesickness would have meant that I would have gone straight back to Dublin. Although Ian Atkins had given me ten games at the end of the previous season, it was Roy that gave me my big chance and I'll always appreciate that.

Introduction

Colchester United faced up to their second season in the GM Vauxhall Conference with major changes in both the boardroom and the manager's hot-seat. The much-lamented Jonathan Crisp had vacated his chair after five years, and been succeeded by local businessman James Bowdidge. Crisp suggested that his original £180,000 outlay for the club had actually cost him £1m of his own money, and his parting shot was that it was 'a bloody disgrace' that full-time Colchester had been pipped by Barnet to the title in the previous season. Bowdidge purchased the controlling interest for 'a nominal sum'. His vow was to return the club to the fans, brushing aside the veil of secrecy that had soured relations between the old board and the supporters.

Former chairman Robert Jackson returned to the club and he was joined by John Worsp and Charlie Simpson as directors. John Schultz, intent on setting up a self-financing youth policy, would also eventually return to the board. Mr Bowdidge's first task was to take down the 'All players available for sale' sign, whilst still acknowledging that incoming transfer fees were the life-blood of small clubs and that the club would strive to produce players who had the ability and desire to play at a higher level. The future of the club, he maintained, lay in collective ownership and commitment from every fan; co-operation with the local authority and with the Colchester public as a whole.

On the pitch, Ian Atkins, who had been player-manager, left to take up a coaching role at Birmingham City. New player-manager Roy McDonough was faced with an immediate problem. With Atkins gone and fellow centre half Scott Daniels transferred to Exeter City, McDonough had a gaping hole in his defensive squad. Before Atkins' departure, U's played three pre-season friendlies – drawing 2-2 with Ipswich, losing 0-3 to Leyton Orient (both behind closed doors) and succumbing to Bury Town by a single goal.

United's first victory came at Sudbury, where goals by McDonough and Nicky Smith earned U's an odd goal in three success. A sloppy defeat by a late goal at Enfield was followed by a 5-3 win at Wivenhoe. Mario Walsh, Tony English, McDonough, Julian Dart and an own goal made up U's quintet. Cornard were seen off by 2-1 with a rare Warren Donald goal and an assist by a home defender.

Facing Third Division side Fulham before an 847 crowd, Gary Bennett's brace earned an encouraging victory, but Second Division Brentford proved too strong in the final warm-up game. The West Londoners cruised to a 3-1 win, after Walsh had given United an interval lead.

The battle for the GM Vauxhall Conference and the prize of a place amongst the Football League elite was ready to commence. Witton Albion, from the HFS Loans League, who had unexpectedly dispatched United from the previous season's FA Trophy

Controversial out-going chairman Jonathon Crisp, who paid £180,000 for control of the club, claimed his tenure in charge had cost over £1,000,000 of his own money and he then sold the club for a 'nominal sum'.

New chairman James Bowdidge vowed to return the club to its rightful owners – the fans.

competition, Farnborough and Redbridge Forest were all newly promoted. Wycombe Wanderers, under former Northern Ireland international Martin O'Neill, were installed as favourites, with U's a close second.

Colchester's abrasive attitude to being 'non-League' would ruffle more than a few feathers in the Conference hierarchy, just as it would in the inner sanctums of Wycombe's Adams Park. The psychological warfare waged between McDonough and O'Neill, with the added interjections of Wanderers' director and television pundit Alan Parry as the title race hotted up, would be matched by a bizarre 'local derby'-style rivalry between the supporters of both clubs, which remains intact today.

ENCOURAGING START FOR COLCHESTER

Saturday 17 August 1991
Referee: Mr C.J. Proud (Finchley)

Colchester 2 Macclesfield 0
Attendance: 2,233

By Neal Manning, *East Anglian Daily Times*

A first-day crowd of over 2,000 was very encouraging and, to a large degree, so was the performance of Colchester United on Saturday as they started their second season in the GM Vauxhall Conference on a winning note. Last season they had to wait until the third match before chalking up their first success, but this time they have been quick off the mark. For new player-manager Roy McDonough, it was a match in which he was involved in the build-up to both goals and also earned himself a booking for dissent. 'I'll settle for that – three points and a clean sheet', said McDonough, who knows full well that there is room for improvement. 'We didn't do as much in Macclesfield's half as we could have done. We found it difficult to get out in the second half against the wind. But if we continue to pass the ball in the way I know we can, then we will create plenty of chances.'

Carbon copy

Saturday's victory was a carbon copy of so many of the U's performances of last season. Having established a 2-0 interval lead, Colchester failed to kill off Macclesfield. The result, however, was never in doubt and Macclesfield's manager Peter Wragg admitted: 'The better side won. Colchester were stronger than us and their goals were at the right time for them.' The performance of Warren Donald, now operating at right-back, was particularly encouraging for the U's. His non-stop display comfortably made him Man of the Match as he did so much good work at both ends of the pitch.

Just reward

The first-half showing by Colchester was excellent, and the two goals they scored were just reward for their effort. The first goal arrived in the tenth minute. Collins chipped the ball forward from midfield for McDonough to run onto. He beat a defender but, as he was about to try a shot, the advancing Farrelly blocked him. The ball, however, flew across the face of goal, where Bennett raced in to open his account for the new campaign. United's second goal in first-half injury time was a real gem. McGavin and Kinsella combined in midfield before the busy little Irishman released the ball to McDonough. With a first-time flick, McDonough touched the ball on for McGavin, who had timed his run to perfection to get behind the Macclesfield defence. The former Sudbury striker, who has been hampered by injury in the pre-season build-up, kept his cool before rounding the advancing goalkeeper and sticking the ball into the empty net. It was a move and finish right out of the top drawer. In the second half, in which Barrett was booked for bringing down substitute Dawson outside the penalty area, the U's went close to increasing their lead, but the quality of their play did not match that of the first forty-five minutes.

The Colchester United squad face the cameras on press day, unaware of the season that will unfold in front of them. From left to right, back row: Steve Foley (coach), Ian Phillips (player-coach), Martin Grainger, Scott Daniels (transferred to Exeter City), Paul Gothard, Scott Barett, Mario Walsh, Tony English, Stuart Bevis (physiotherapist), Roy Mcdonough (player-manager). Front row: Steve McGavin, Mark Kinsella, Nicky Smith, Warren Donald, Steve Restarick, Gary Bennett, Shaun Elliott, Eamonn Collins.

Colchester: Barrett, Donald, Grainger, Kinsella, English, Elliott, Collins, Bennett, McDonough, McGavin (*sub* Walsh 76), Smith. *Unused sub:* Goodwin.
Macclesfield: S. Farrelly, Shepherd, Johnson (*sub* M. Farrelly 83), Edwards, Tobin, Hanlon, Askey, Dempsey, Lambert, Clayton (*sub* Dawson 55).

COLCHESTER FAIL TO TURN PRESSURE INTO GOALS

Saturday 24 August 1991
Referee: Mr R. Poulain (Huddersfield)

Barrow 1 Colchester 1
Attendance: 1,480

From the *East Anglian Daily Times*

Peter McDonnell is a name that will long be etched in the memory of Steve McGavin. The Colchester striker must have thought his goal-bound header from six yards out was points in the bag for the promotion-chasing outfit. But no one had told the Barrow 'keeper that, and he pulled off a tremendous save in the eightieth minute to ensure his side finished with a share of the spoils. However, Colchester must have wondered on the long journey back home how they failed to turn pressure into goals in a sparkling first half. The U's simply dominated the opening forty-five minutes, but the only reward they received was a goal in the thirtieth minute netted by Mark Kinsella, who rifled the ball home from twenty yards.

Telling breaks

Even after the interval, when they had to soak up a lot of pressure, Colchester made a couple of telling breaks but again failed to capitalise on their chances. Colchester could have gone ahead as early as the second minute when a half-chance fell to McGavin, whose first time effort finished over the bar but, in spite of all their early probing, the visitors' strike force found a solid obstacle in the form of Gary Messenger, who was the steel in Barrow's defensive spine. The Cumbrians were allowed a brief respite in that first half with Neil Doherty making some headway. However, his two efforts gave the ever-present Scott Barrett few problems. Then the match was held up in the Colchester half for three minutes when referee Richard Poulain first ordered Eamonn Collins and then player-coach Roy McDonough to put on shin pads and abide by last season's rule, but the stoppage failed to halt Colchester's flow and soon after they went ahead through Kinsella, following a measured build-up. Barrow came out after the interval in a determined mood and drew level in the forty-ninth minute when Neil Doherty's near-post corner found Colin Cowperthwaite, who forced the ball home from close range. Cowperthwaite found the back of the net again in the sixty-eighth minute, but his effort was ruled out because of an infringement on the 'keeper by another player. McDonough had a chance to put the visitors ahead when a delightful cross from the left fell in his path near the goal, only to drill his effort wide. Two players were booked – Warren Donald for a foul on Doherty in the fifth minute and Keith McNall in the thirty-seventh minute for an unfair challenge on Barrett, who had pleaded to the referee for leniency for the Barrow striker. But the match was anything but ill-tempered. In fact, quite the opposite, as both sides delivered an abundance of entertainment at Holker Street.

Coach Ian Philips (left) and Steve Foley (above), both valuable 'eyes and ears' for player-manager Roy McDonough.

Barrow: McDonnell, Doolan, Chilton, Skivington, Messenger, Slater, Ballantyne, McNall, Cowperthwaite, Proctor, Doherty. *Unused subs:* Brown, Atkinson.
Colchester: Barrett, Donald, Grainger, Kinsella, English, Elliott, Collins, Bennett, McDonough, McGavin, Smith. *Unused subs:* Phillips, Gray.

FOUR-GOAL McDONOUGH RE-WRITES RECORDS

Monday 26 August 1991
Referee: Mr P. Taylor (Cheshunt)

Slough Town 2 Colchester United 4
Attendance: 2,226

By Neal Manning, *East Anglian Daily Times*

Colchester United's player-coach Roy McDonough wrote himself into the record books with a four-goal salvo before half-time in last night's incident-packed GM Vauxhall Conference match at the Wexham Park Stadium. In an incredible first half, McDonough gave the U's a fourth-minute lead, only for overnight leaders Slough Town to quickly establish a 2-1 advantage. Then McDonough scored three more inside seventeen minutes to put United in the driving seat. The drama spilled into injury time when Slough striker Gary Donnellan was sent off for elbowing Elliott in the face. McDonough became the fourth U's player to score four goals in a match, equalling the feat of Martyn King and Bobby Hunt in a 9-1 win against Bradford almost thirty years ago, and Bobby Svarc at Chester in 1973.

Incident

McDonough had an early second-half chance to score a fifth goal on a night when the U's finishing matched their approach work. There was no way that the second half could have lived up to what had gone before, but it still had its fair share of incident as Slough battled gamely with ten men. Although McDonough grabbed the glory, the man alongside him, Steve McGavin, was particularly impressive and had a hand in three of the goals. The large holiday crowd did not have to wait long for the first-half goal glut to begin. McDonough opened his account with a near-post header after McGavin had headed back a Collins cross and Bennett had had a shot parried by Bunting. The ball spun into the air and McDonough supplied the finishing touch. Two minutes later, the U's were back to square one. Grainger failed to clear the ball and Thompson raced to the byline before cutting back a cross for O'Connor to stroke it past Barrett. Worse was to follow for Colchester, as Slough went ahead in the twelfth minute with Thompson's third goal in as many games. Donnellan made a strong run into the penalty area, but when the U's failed to clear, Thompson picked up the loose ball and turned sharply before sending a low shot past Barrett. United were on terms in the twenty-fourth minute, McDonough heading home Smith's inswinging corner from close range. Four minutes later, McDonough completed his hat-trick. McGavin hit the underside of the bar with a tremendous left foot shot from all of thirty yards. The ball bounced down off the woodwork and McDonough scored easily from virtually on the goal-line. Great play by McGavin in the forty-first minute led to McDonough's and the U's fourth goal. After collecting the ball on the left, he got to the by-line and, despite the close attentions of Stacey, he whipped over a low cross, which McDonough converted with a diving header. McDonough took a knock just below his right eye in scoring this brave goal and for the whole of the second half he had

Slough Town v. Colchester United

United's player-manager Roy McDonough celebrates after scoring.

to use a sponge to try to stem the flow of blood from the wound. Slough's hopes were effectively ended in the second minute of injury time when Donnellan elbowed Elliott in the face right in front of the referee. He was immediately sent off. McDonough should have made it five in the fifty-first minute when, after receiving a pass in an unmarked position from Bennett, he lobbed the advancing goalkeeper, but the ball bounced just past the far post. A diving save by Bunting denied Kinsella in the second half, with the U's defending well against a Slough side who did not throw in the towel. Thompson was booked for a foul on Donald in the fifty-sixth minute to add to the first-half caution of Stacey for a bad challenge on Smith. With eight minutes left, the U's gave Abrahams his first taste of senior football in place of McGavin. Earlier in the half, Phillips had replaced Elliott. So, it was a highly satisfactory night for the U's as they maintained their unbeaten start to the new season – and a personal triumph for Roy McDonough.

Slough: Bunting, Stacey, Pluckrose, Hill, Putman, Turkington (*sub* Stanley 82), Fielder, McKinnon, Donnellan, Thompson, O'Connor. *Unused sub:* Anderson.
Colchester: Barrett, Donald, Grainger, Kinsella, English, Elliott (*sub* Phillips 66), Collins, Bennett, McDonough, McGavin (*sub* Abrahams 82), Smith.

TWO OF THE BEST BY McGAVIN FOR U'S

Saturday 31 August 1991
Referee: Mr M.A. Hair (Peterborough)

Colchester 5 Bath City 0
Attendance: 2,416

From the *East Anglian Daily Times*

If Steve McGavin continues to score goals like the two he netted at Layer Road on Saturday, Colchester United will have a prize asset on their hands. McGavin's finishing was right out of the top drawer and reminiscent of former Ipswich Town striker Alan Brazil in his heyday of ten years ago. You would have had to go a long way to see a better goal than McGavin's second in the fifty-first minute, as United chalked up their biggest victory since they became members of the Vauxhall Conference. After McDonough had flicked on a long clearance from Barrett, McGavin brought the ball down with his left foot and, in one movement, turned and volleyed it into the corner of the net. It was a quite stunning goal to add to his twenty-eighth minute opener.

Proved the master

Just as he did on the first day of the season against Macclesfield, McGavin proved the master in a one-on-one situation with the goalkeeper. Running onto a through-ball from Smith past a hesitant Bath defence, McGavin dropped his shoulder and left Churchward on the ground before firing into the net. It was just like shelling peas, and certainly comparable with Brazil at his best. 'Scoring like that is all about confidence,' said McGavin. Twelve goals from their first four matches is a very satisfying return, with the three U's strikers scoring eleven of them. There was a first ever hat-trick for Gary Bennett, who left the ground all smiles and with the match ball safely tucked under his arm. Whereas Roy McDonough had to pay £30 to buy the ball with which he scored four goals at Slough the previous Monday, there was no charge to Bennett. It was certainly a highly satisfactory afternoon's work for the U's, but Ian Phillips, player-coach McDonough's assistant, refuses to get carried away. He said, 'We're not firing on all cylinders yet, but at least we're still winning. What really pleases me is the work rate and the fact everybody is pulling for one another. The spirit is brilliant.' Phillips, for one, will not allow anybody to get carried away with this more than encouraging start to a new season. Championships are not won in August, but certainly the quality of the U's play on Saturday has given food for thought. Bath's player-manager, Tony Ricketts, was suitably impressed, despite being on the wrong end of a heavy defeat. He said: 'Colchester are one of the best sides I have ever seen in the Conference. Their running off the ball and organization was superb.' It did, however, take the first goal to really get the U's going but after that there was only one team in it. After McGavin's opener, two more goals quickly followed to condemn Bath to an afternoon of torture. Bennett's first in the thirty-second minute was a case of being in the right place at the right time after McGavin's mis-kick had fallen to him at the far post. Bennett's finish for the second and Colchester's third was clinical. He volleyed into the roof of the net after McDonough had flicked a Collins free-kick across the face of goal. Bennett completed his hat-trick three minutes from time, heading firmly past Churchward after

Above: Steve McGavin, as elusive as ever, opened the scoring against Bath City at Layer Road. *Right:* Gary Bennett completes his hat-trick in the 5-0 rout of Bath City, with Paul Abrahams in attendence.

another long clearance from Barrett had looped in the air off a Bath defender. While Bennett and McGavin grabbed the glory, it was a good all-round team performance in which Kinsella continued to stamp his authority on the midfield. Kinsella, unfortunate not to have a run last season, is certainly now proving his weight in gold and is just one reason why the U's have got off to the start they wanted.

Colchester: Barrett, Donald, Grainger, Kinsella, English, Elliott, Collins, Bennett, McDonough (*sub* Abrahams 74), McGavin, Smith. *Unused sub:* Phillips.
Bath: Churchward, Hedges, Payne, Singleton, Crowley (*sub* Ricketts 65), Radford, Banks, Brown, Withey, Randall (*sub* Painter 72), Boyle.

BARRETT SAVES U'S

Saturday 7 September 1991
Referee: Mr K. Whittaker (Bolton)

Witton Albion 2 Colchester 2
Attendance: 1,045

By Neal Manning, *East Anglian Daily Times*

Defensive lapses proved costly for Colchester United at Wincham Park on Saturday, even though they maintained their unbeaten start to the season. The U's gifted Conference new boys Witton Albion both their goals before Scott Barrett, last season's Player of the Year, came to the rescue in the last minute. Barrett, who earned something like a dozen points on his own in the U's first year in the Conference, dived to his right to deny Witton substitute McCluskie with a fine save with only seconds remaining. Colchester's defence, which had looked none too secure when put under pressure; was prised open alarmingly by McCluskie's jinking run, and it was just as well that the reliable Barrett came to the rescue. Although a draw was the right result on the balance of play, the U's player-coach Roy McDonough said: 'Two bad goals cost us the match. Our lack of quality in the last third of the pitch also let us down. Witton were a well-organized side and were prepared to try and play football, but I felt we created the better chances.' The U's, however, can feel disappointed that they did not do better and in some areas there appeared to be a lack of urgency. One or two players were rarely seen in the last half-hour as the hot sun sapped their energy. Peter O'Brien, who took over at Witton just before the start of the season, said: 'Overall we've got to be pleased. Both sides had half-a-dozen chances and took two each, but it was a very good save by their 'keeper at the death that prevented us winning.'

Unchallenged

Colchester, who have a chance to close the gap on 100 per cent leaders Wycombe tomorrow night when they meet Farnborough at Layer Road, fell behind to a well-worked free-kick by Witton in the nineteenth minute. After Elliott had been penalised for a foul midway inside his own half, Witton opened up the U's defence who failed to pick up Thomas as he converted Lutkevitch's cross unchallenged from close in. Defensive deficiencies also showed up again on the hour when Ellis headed Witton's equalizer. McDonough took the blame for jumping too early when Stewart floated over a free-kick from the right, but Ellis could not believe how much space he had been left as he headed just inside Barrett's right-hand upright. In between Witton's goals, the U's had scored two good ones themselves with a first of the season for Collins and McDonough's fifth of the campaign. Eight minutes after Witton had taken the lead, a long throw from Grainger on the left was flicked on by McDonough. McGavin tried a shot in a crowded penalty area before the ball came out to Collins on the edge of the box and the little Irishman hammered a low right-foot shot beyond Mason's reach. Colchester's second goal came within two minutes of the start of the second half. A surging forward run by Bennett ended with him crashing a tremendous twenty-five-yard drive against the bar. The ball rebounded into the

Right: Nicky Smith and Martin Graianger combine to foil a Witton Albion attack at Wincham Park.

Below: Colchester United goalkeeper Scott Barrett is powerless to prevent Witton's Karl Thomas from scoring in the 2-2 draw on Saturday

path of McDonough, who coolly side-footed home, much to the delight of the travelling fans, many of whom had arrived only just before the start of the match after being held up on the M6 by roadworks. Grainger was booked for a heavy challenge on the dangerous Connor in the sixty-second minute and, fourteen minutes later, he limped off with a recurrence of a bruised instep. The young defender is doubtful for tomorrow's match. Phillips, who would have been a natural replacement, is ruled out for at least another month after undergoing a minor operation for a torn cartilage. On the way home from Cheshire, the BBC Radio 5 presenter announced that Wycombe might as well be given the Conference title after winning their first six matches. Remember Kettering's flying start to last season when they were more than a dozen points clear of the chasing pack? There is a long way to go yet, but the U's can help themselves if they cut out those defensive lapses.

Witton Albion: Mason, Stewart, Coathup, McNeil, Ellis (*sub* McCluskie 76), Anderson, Thomas (*sub* Edwards 79), Lodge, Lutkevitch, Cuddy, Connor.
Colchester: Barrett, Donald, Grainger (*sub* Goodwin 76), Kinsella, English, Elliott, Collins, Bennett, McDonough, McGavin, Smith. *Unused sub:* Abrahams.

DEFENSIVE SLIPS COST U'S DEAR

Tuesday 10 September 1991　　　　**Colchester 2 Farnborough Town 3**
Referee: Mr W.J. Norbury (Harlow)　　Attendance: 2,954

By Neal Manning, *East Anglian Daily Times*

Colchester United committed defensive suicide before the best crowd of the season at Layer Road last night and it enabled Farnborough to maintain their 100 per cent away record. The U's handed the Hampshire side two goals on a plate as Farnborough romped to their fourth successive away win – and they could even afford the luxury of missing a penalty. Add the two goals they conceded at Witton Albion on Saturday and it means that the U's have let in five in their last 180 minutes of football – certainly not Championship form. A great deal of work will have to be done before the U's meet Yeovil at Layer Road on Friday night. The individual mistakes by Grainger and Elliott took the gloss off a high quality GM Vauxhall Conference match in which the first half, in particular, was a real credit to the League.

Clinical

The U's played some cracking football in that first period but still found themselves trailing at the interval. In the second half, the home side were disappointing and a lack of bite in midfield put pressure on the defence which did not stand up too well against the fast-breaking Farnborough. The Conference new boys certainly made Colchester pay for their lapses. Clinical finishing accounted for their three goals – and apart from the penalty miss they were the only serious shots they had all night. Colchester's unbeaten start to the season attracted the scouts to Layer Road. Five First Division clubs were represented including Liverpool, Spurs and West Ham, but the evening went rather flat from a home point of view. A late goal from Collins sparked off a rousing finale – Elliott had a header blocked on the line – but the U's were unable to salvage anything from the defensive debris. It was all go from the first minute when Kinsella saw a shot bounce off Power's body. Collins was booked for dissent before Farnborough took the lead in the ninth minute. Coombs picked up the ball just inside the U's half and ran forward unchallenged before beating the diving Barrett with a left-foot shot from twenty-five yards. United's pressure paid off with a twenty-first-minute equaliser through McGavin. A Collins chip was turned behind by Baker from Smith's corner to beyond the far post, and Bennett knocked the ball back for McGavin to volley into the roof of the net for his fourth of the season. Donald was only just off target soon afterwards with a cracking thirty-five-yard shot and although McDonough had the ball in the Farnborough net in the thirty-eighth minute it was disallowed because the referee judged he had fouled the goalkeeper. In the last minute of what had been a tremendous half, a bad mistake by Grainger allowed Farnborough to regain the lead. He failed to clear the ball and Rogers made ground before crossing to Read, who curled a left-foot shot beyond Barrett and into the far corner of the net. Farnborough had the chance to make certain of the points in the fifty-eighth minute

20

COLCHESTER v. FARNBOROUGH TOWN

Left: Steve McGavin and Nicky Smith win this aerial duel against Farnborough. *Right:* Only the cross bar prevented this Eamonn Collins' free-kick from earning U's a point against Farnborough.

when Donald brought down Coombs in tbe penalty area. A long clearance from Baker had bounced over the U's defence, but Coombs was yards offside when Read touched the ball through to him. Justice was done, however, when Coombs drove the spot-kick yards wide of Barrett's left hand.

Advancing

Six minutes later and the U's had another escape when McDonough appeared to punch a cross from Read in the box but it escaped the referee's attention. Farnborough made amends for their penalty miss by scoring a third goal in the sixty-seventh minute, and it was the result of another bad mistake. Elliott, with time to clear from inside his own half, slipped and presented Read with an opening. The Farnborough striker burst clear before finishing with a right-foot shot past the advancing Barrett. In the closing stages, with the U's trying to recover lost ground, Collins was unlucky in the seventy-ninth minute when his free-kick hit the bar but, seven minutes later, he reduced the arrears when his shot from inside the penalty area, following a corner, trickled into the net. That set up an exciting finish, but the U's just failed to break down the visitor's defence.

Colchester: Barrett, Donald, Grainger, Kinsella, English, Elliott, Collins, Bennett, McDonough, McGavin, Smith. *Unused subs:* Goodwin, Abrahams.
Farnborough: Power, Holmes, Baker, Broome, Bye, Wigmore, Rogers, Doherty, Coombs (*sub* Lovell 77), Read, Horton. *Unused sub:* Stevens.

U'S FINALLY FIND THEIR BEST FORM

Friday 13 September 1991　　　　**Colchester 4 Yeovil Town 0**
Referee: Mr I.M.D. Mitchell　　　　Attendance: 2,979
　　　　　(West Wickham)

By Neal Manning, *East Anglian Daily Times*

It took some considerable time for Colchester United to get going at Layer Road last night, but once they took the lead just before half-time, there was no stopping them. Tony English's first goal of the season, in the forty-first minute, gave the U's a lead they hardly deserved. In the second half, however, it was a different story as United played some fine attacking football, and two further goals by the fifty-sixth minute put the match well beyond Yeovil's reach. After that there was only one team in it, as the U's bombarded the Somerset side – who had doubled them last season – and with McGavin leading their defence a merry dance, Yeovil were fortunate only to concede one further goal. Colchester took their tally to twenty goals for the season in seven matches and now have Bennett on six and McGavin and McDonough with five apiece. After conceding two goals in their previous two matches, the U's will be pleased to have kept a clean sheet.

Guns blazing

In the first half, Yeovil were the better side for long periods but without doing any damage to the U's defence. McGavin's thirty-second-minute effort was the only one Colchester had on target until English opened the scoring. Donald engineered the opening from the right, and after McDonough had knocked down his cross from the right, English was on hand to pick up the loose ball and fire it into the empty net. The U's came out for the second half with all guns blazing, and in the fifty-first minute they increased their lead through Bennett. Smith crossed low from the left and Bennett brought the ball under control before firing a left-foot shot that Fry allowed to slip through his hands. Five minutes later and the cock-a-hoop U's scored again. A corner from Collins on the left was headed down by Grainger, and McGavin hit a rasping drive that Fry got a hand to, but could not prevent from going into the net. Yeovil missed an opportunity to pull a goal back in the fifty-ninth minute when Spencer raced through only to shoot hopelessly wide. Colchester were really bubbling up at this stage and every time McGavin had the ball something was likely to happen. In the sixty-seventh minute, he turned inside on the right and his shot went off Rutter and hit the post. Bennett squandered a good chance from close in with his shot hitting a defender before Smith, still searching for his first goal since joining the club at the start of last season, headed just over from Kinsella's pinpoint cross. There was a spate of bookings as this now one-sided match drew to a close. Player-coach McDonough received his second caution of the season for a foul, before Yeovil pair Ferns and substitute McEvoy both went into the referee's notebook for fouls on Donald and Smith respectively. The U's thoroughly deserved their fourth goal in the third minute of injury time. Kinsella ploughed his way into the penalty area before picking out Bennett

High fives for Steve McGavin and Tony English following the skipper's 41st-minute opener against Yeovil Town at Layer Road.

with a good cross, and the little striker was left with the easiest of chances to head the ball home with the Yeovil defence all at sixes and sevens. So a week which started with a disappointing home defeat by Farnborough ended with the U's in top gear, boosting their goal tally into the bargain.

Colchester: Barrett, Donald, Grainger, Kinsella, English, Elliott, Collins, Bennett, McDonough, McGavin, Smith. *Unused subs:* Goodwin, Abrahams.

Yeovil: Fry, Harrower (*sub* McDermott 55), Ferns, Shail, Rutter, Cooper, Carroll, Batty, Pritchard (*sub* McEvoy 81), Spencer, Colling.

STRAIGHT TALKING FOR U'S PLAYERS

Saturday 21 September 1991
Referee: Mr K.A. Leach (Birmingham)

Cheltenham Town 1 Colchester 1
Attendance: 1,157

By Neal Manning, *East Anglian Daily Times*

The sort of performance that Colchester United turned in against Cheltenham at Whaddon Road on Saturday certainly won't be tolerated again. Chairman James Bowdidge was clearly unhappy with what he saw, while player-coach Roy McDonough and his number two, Ian Phillips, were both bitterly disappointed, to say the least, about a match the U's should have won. There will be some straight talking during the coming week to make sure there is no repeat if Colchester are to hold realistic hopes of winning the GM Vauxhall Conference title. Phillips, who on the touchline was almost tearing out what little hair he has left, said: 'Some players went into the game with the wrong attitude. They didn't put themselves about and were happy to sit in and hide. We gave the ball away too much and what really disappointed me was the final pass. You can't turn football on and off like taps – you've got to earn the right to beat the opposition.' An uneven and bumpy pitch did not help the players' cause, but Phillips did not offer that as an excuse. He said: 'Teams like Cheltenham work on one long ball to try and do the damage because they're not good enough to win from open play. When we're passing the ball, we're better than any other teams in this league, but on Saturday we let ourselves down.' Phillips also finds it frustrating that some of the younger players cannot keep up a level of consistency, but insists that every player should have pride in his performance. The absence of Steve McGavin with a slight Achilles injury was a blow – he'll be fit for next Saturday's match at Wycombe – but even without him the U's should have gone on to win the game after taking a thirteenth-minute lead with McDonough's sixth goal of the season. 'You won't see a better goal all season,' said Phillips. McDonough volleyed a Collins cross over the 'keeper and into the far corner of the net. After that cracking goal, it was down to the U's who continued to frustrate their large number of travelling supporters by failing to provide the right final ball when Cheltenham were stretched at the back and looked there for the taking. Many teams in the Conference rely on scoring goals from set pieces, and this is an area in which the U's have proved vulnerable this season. Cheltenham's fortieth-minute equalizer resulted from a free-kick that was pumped into the penalty area and Owen, after picking up a knockdown, made a space for himself before firing a close-range left-foot shot into the roof of the net. In McGavin's absence, the U's reverted to a 4-4-2 line-up, with Gray coming in at right-back for his debut with Donald pushing forward to the right-hand side of midfield. That left just McDonough, who was booked on the stroke of half-time for a foul, and Bennett up front. In the second half, the U's had their chances of scoring further goals but lack of quality with the final ball meant that the Cheltenham 'keeper was not really put to the test. Colchester did have

Above: Midfielder Mark Kinsella, in typically commanding style, shows why he was selected for the Republic of Ireland's Under-21 clash with Turkey. *Right:* Paul Abrahams, a young hopeful on the fringe of the first team.

an escape in the sixty-fifth minute when Purdie hit the post, and again in injury time, when Buckland was allowed a free header following a free-kick but, fortunately, the ball went straight to Barrett. English and Elliott will be absolved from any criticism as they fought hard throughout in the heart of the defence. Otherwise, it was a performance that the U's will want to forget on a day when leaders Wycombe lost for the first time and the chance to close the gap was squandered.

Cheltenham: M. Barrett, Butler, Willets, Owen, Vircavs, Brogan, Brooks (*sub* Reck 59), Stobart, Buckland, Casey, Purdie. *Unused sub:* Bloomfield.
Colchester: S. Barrett, Donald, Grainger, Kinsella, English, Elliott, Collins, Bennett, McDonough, Gray, Smith. *Unused subs:* Abrahams, Goodwin.

BARRETT TO THE RESCUE IN VITAL UNITED VICTORY

Saturday 28 September 1991
Referee: Mr C.R. Wilkes (Gloucester)

Wycombe Wanderers 1 Colchester 2
Attendance: 5,186

By Neal Manning, *East Anglian Daily Times.*

For Nicky Smith and Scott Barrett, Saturday's top-of-the-table GM Vauxhall Conference clash at Adams Park will long remain in the memory. Smith's first goal since he joined Colchester United at the start of last season was long overdue, but for a goalkeeper to score is a rarity. With the seconds ticking away, Barrett launched a long clearance and the ball bounced in the Wycombe penalty area and over the heads of Creaser and Hyde into the net. 'I thought it was an own goal', said Barrett, 'but then all the lads came rushing back to congratulate me and I realised the ball had gone straight in.'

Training paid off

It was an unexpected bonus for the U's, with a draw looking the likely outcome, but there was no doubt that Roy McDonough's side deserved a victory. 'A great team performance', said McDonough's number two Ian Phillips, who had been rightly critical of the display at Cheltenham seven days earlier. 'We defended exceptionally well in the first half, and in the last twenty minutes, I thought Wycombe began to tire and our full-time training paid off.' Despite the awful weather conditions, the 5,186 crowd – the biggest for a Conference match this season – had to endure a dull first half, but got full value for the excitement provided in the final forty-five minutes. There was understandable jubilation from the U's players and around 1,000 travelling supporters. But for Wycombe, who suffered their second home defeat in a week, it was a day of disbelief and bitter disappointment. Well-known television commentator Alan Parry, who is a director of Wycombe, was in no doubt that the U's deserved their success. He said: 'So many teams come here solely intent in trying to get a draw, but Colchester went all out for victory right to the end. I was impressed by them.' In the first half, U's had to defend in depth against a gale-force wind and driving rain and restricted Wycombe to a couple of good scoring chances. New signing Roberts settled in well in his sweeper's role, while Donald and Smith did good jobs to cut out the threat of Guppy and Carroll. It was certainly not a match for the faint-hearted, with challenges flying in thick and fast, but there were far too many stoppages and, as a result, there was little flow to the first half. In the third minute of stoppage time, McDonough, with six away goals already under his belt this season, was set up by McGavin, but his shot came down off the underside of the bar. The second half was only four minutes old when Smith struck with a goal that he will always remember. Good work by Donald set up the chance and Smith's finishing was clinical, with a left-foot shot that flew into the top corner of the net from the edge of the penalty area. Smith, who could have had a hat-trick in the corresponding game last season, virtually did a lap of honour to celebrate the goal that had been long coming. With the U's now poised to go on and

Wycombe Wanderers v. Colchester

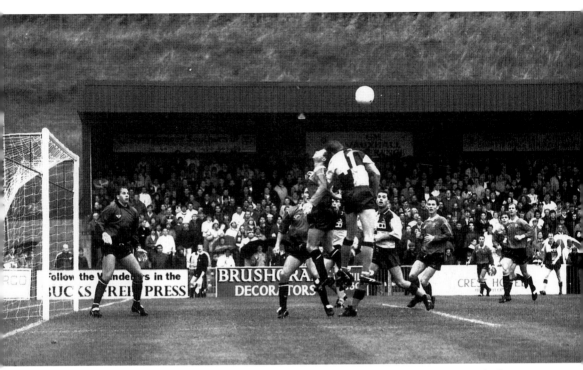

Scott Barrett is an imposing figure in the Colchester goal as his defenders cope with the challenge of Wycombe left-winger Steve Guppy

collect maximum points, they were rocked by Wycombe's fifty-seventh-minute equalizer, which should have never been allowed. Nuttell clearly fouled Barrett as he tried to punch clear Cousins' teasing cross. The ball fell to Guppy, who calmly lobbed it over Barrett and into the net. The linesman had been flagging for an infringement the moment it happened, but the referee, after lengthy consultation, overruled him. The U's lost their impetus for a while after this, but the introduction of Cook, signed on loan from Southend last week, in place of the injured Kinsella, kept them going. Although the U's finished the stronger, it took Barrett's freak goal to settle the issue, and they should have had a penalty soon afterwards when McGavin was brought down by Kerr. Once again, the standard of refereeing left a great deal to be desired. Referee Wilkes booked five players, three from Colchester – Bennett and McDonough (fouls) and Collins (dissent) – with McDonough particularly unlucky as he collected his third caution of the season.

Wycombe: Hyde, Cousins, Crossley, Kerr, Creaser, G. Smith, Carroll, Stapleton (*sub* Scott 83), West (*sub* Hutchinson 83), Nuttell, Guppy.
Colchester: Barrett, Donald, Roberts, Kinsella (*sub* Cook 69), English, Elliott, Collins, Bennett, McDonough, McGavin, Smith. *Unused sub:* Grainger.

SET PIECES SPOIL U'S GOOD WORK

Saturday 5 October 1991
Referee: Mr G. Poll (Berkhampstead)

Colchester 3 Altrincham 3
Attendance: 2,149

By Neal Manning, *East Anglian Daily Times.*

Until Colchester United learn to deal with set pieces, there will be more trouble ahead, judging by the way they surrendered the lead three times at Layer Road on Saturday. For the second time in only five home matches, they have conceded three goals, and against Altrincham it was a case of after the Lord Mayor's Show, following the dramatic last-minute victory at Wycombe seven days earlier. From the U's point of view, they gave away two goals of schoolboy proportions in a somewhat crazy game in which referee Graham Poll angered players and spectators alike by giving two controversial penalties and booking five players, all for trivial offences. It was all the more disappointing for Colchester after a sparkling opening twenty minutes. Altrincham successfully closed down the U's in the second half, and they were unable to create in the manner in which they did before the interval. Ian Phillips, number two to player-coach Roy McDonough, said, 'We are still seeking a level of consistency. But there is no way you should lose at home when you score three goals. With all their goals coming from set pieces, it is an area we will have to work on.' The U's took their goals tally to twenty-six in just ten matches, but this impressive record will stand for nothing if they continue to give them away at the other end. The marking was non-existent for Altrincham's first two goals. Three minutes after Colchester had taken the lead, McKenna was allowed an unchallenged shot in the penalty area from Brady's corner and his left-foot volley flew into the net. Altrincham's second goal five minutes into the second half was horrific from the U's point of view. Anderson's free-kick from more than midway inside the home half took one bounce before whipping off the surface into the net. Rowlands claimed that he had got a touch, but afterwards it was confirmed that the ball had gone straight into the net, which made it an even worse goal to concede. When the U's had gone into a sixteenth-minute lead, it was no more than they deserved. Collins put Bennett away on the right, and when he cut the ball back, Anderson was at full stretch in attempting to clear, only to steer it into the bottom corner of the net. McGavin's sixth goal of the season in the thirty-fifth minute had put the U's back in front, and again their attacking first-half display had warranted them restoring their lead. Roberts, making his home debut, saw his long throw from the right flicked on by McDonough. The ball fell to Bennett, who steered it out of Wealand's grasp and into the path of McGavin, who converted the simplest of opportunities. When the U's were awarded a seventieth-minute penalty after Anderson was penalised for handling the ball, it threw the home side a lifeline. Altrincham were understandably upset at the decision, but McDonough restored the lead for the third time with an excellent kick, low into the bottom corner for his seventh goal of the season and his first at home. Six minutes later, McDonough was penalised for a nudge on Rowlands on the half-way line, and even Altrincham manager Stan Allen admitted that it did not warrant a free-kick. Anderson

Roy McDonough and Altrincham defender Paul Rowlands give chase, with a sparsely populated Clock End in their wake.

curled the ball over and, when McDonough climbed above Rowlands, referee Poll immediately pointed to the spot, indicating that the U's player-coach had impeded the Robins' defender. Brady's spot-kick was a poor one and, although Barrett got his hands to the ball, he was visibly upset that he was unable to prevent it from crossing the line. Four Altrincham players – McKenna, Daws, Rowland, and Hughes – and Colchester's Bennett were all booked on the day when the yellow card came back into operation in the Conference for the first time for six years. Now the U's have an early opportunity to get Saturday's game out of their systems when they meet Kettering tomorrow in the second round of the Bob Lord Trophy at Layer Road.

Colchester: Barrett, Donald, Roberts, Kinsella, English, Elliott, Collins, Bennett, McDonough, McGavin, Smith. *Unused subs:* Grainge, Cook.
Altrincham: Wealands, Edwards, Densmore, Rowlands, Reid, Anderson, Rudge, Dews, Grady, Hughes (*sub* Lewis 37), McKenna. *Unused sub:* Wiggins.

EMPHATIC VICTORY FOR UNITED

Tuesday 8 October 1991

Referee: Mr G.C. Monk (Grays)

Colchester 4 Kettering Town 0
(Bob Lord Trophy First Round)
Attendance: 1,289

By Neal Manning, *East Anglian Daily Times*

Colchester United reached the third round of the Bob Lord Trophy with an emphatic victory over Conference rivals Kettering last night. First-half goals from McGavin and Collins paved the way before substitute Kinsella scored twice after coming on for the last half-hour. The U's, showing three changes in the starting line-up from Saturday's 3-3 draw with Altrincham, had few problems with Collins pulling the strings in midfield for an hour before he gave way to Kinsella. McGavin opened the scoring with his seventh goal of the season in the sixteenth minute – and what a peach it was. Collins knocked the ball forward and McGavin, showing superb close skills, outstripped Kettering's two central defenders before rounding Bastock and sticking the ball in the net.

Handicapped

Kettering, so square at the back, were handicapped when Slack limped off in the thirty-first minute. On the stroke of half-time, the U's increased their lead through Collins. McGavin and Smith combined on the left before Smith picked out the unmarked Collins at the far post, and the little midfield player headed easily past Bastock. Abrahams and Kinsella were introduced on the hour for Duffett, the nineteen-year-year-old non-contract striker given his senior opportunity, and Collins. Kinsella and Cook both went close before Kinsella scored the U's third goal in the seventy-fourth minute, heading home after a Bennett shot had looped up off the 'keeper. Six minutes from time, Kinsella side-footed the ball home after Bennett had pulled it back from the byline.

Colchester: Barrett, Donald, Grainger, Cook, English, Roberts, Collins (*sub* Kinsella 60), Bennett, Duffett (*sub* Abrahams 60), McGavin, Smith.
Kettering: Bastock, Price, Jones, Nicol, Slack (*sub* Christie 31), Bloodworth, Graham, Brown, Cotton, Bancroft, Appleby. *Unused sub:* Reddin.

Scott Barrett soaks up the adulation from the huge U's following after his 89th –minute drop-kick had sailed over Wycombe keeper Paul Hyde's head and into the net to give United a vital 2-1 win at Adams Park.

Roy McDonough and the Wycombe defence stall in anticipation as the Colchester player-manager's effort goes narrowly wide of the Wycombe goal.

DISPUTED PENALTY SAVES COLCHESTER

Saturday 12 October 1991
Referee: Mr A.D. Danskin
(Leigh-on-Sea)

Colchester 2 Runcorn 1
Attendance: 2,617

By Neal Manning, *East Anglian Daily Times*

If Colchester United had accepted a percentage of the clearcut chances they created at Layer Road on Saturday, there would have been no need for the blatant time-wasting tactics of Runcorn or the late decider from a hotly disputed penalty. The U's left behind their shooting boots – Gary Bennett in particular – but in the end, all was well, when player-coach Roy McDonough blasted home his eighth goal of the season with four minutes of normal time remaining. It was, however, no more than Colchester deserved. They had been on top for most of a match that was never allowed to flow because of rugged Runcorn's antics.

Lenient referee

The referee was lenient to the visitors until he became a friend to the frustrated home supporters by throwing the U's a lifeline, just when they looked to be chucking away a match they should have had wrapped up long before the end. When Smith crossed from the left, Collins went down in the penalty area unchallenged. Runcorn were furious and their player-manager John Carroll said: 'The referee gave what he saw, but it was a pity that a goal like that should decide the outcome. The lad admitted that he conned the referee.' Justice was, in many ways, done when McDonough stepped up to score from the spot, minutes after Palladino had infuriated the crowd by claiming he had been felled by a missile. That provoked yet another lengthy stoppage, and the referee added more than five minutes of extra time.

Left door open

Ian Phillips, who runs a critical eye over the U's from the dugout, said: 'In the end, we were glad of the three points. Overall, we were not bad and, at times, we really had to scrap it out. By failing to take our chances, we left the door open for Runcorn and then we gave away a bad goal.' The lowly Cheshire side, who had few goal-scoring opportunities, should have taken a nineteenth-minute lead when Shaughnessy miskicked with the goal at his mercy and, three minutes later, Bennett did likewise after being set up by McGavin. Chances continued to go begging until Bennett made amends for his earlier miss by breaking the deadlock in the fifty-second minute with his seventh goal of the season. Bennett converted McGavin's cross at the far post, following a move that had been started by Donald. Colchester certainly will not be happy with Runcorn's equalising goal in the sixty-ninth minute. Brabin's long throw was flicked on by Shaughnessy and fell to full-back Redmond. He was able to get in a shot unchallenged that rebounded off the post. It looked as though Smith, in trying to clear, put the

No way through Runcorn's defence for Colchester captain Tony English at Layer Road. The U's finally broke the Cheshire side's stubbornness with an 86th minute penalty from Roy McDonough.

rebound into his own net, but Redmond claimed he got the last touch and no one was prepared to argue with that. Barrett, who had a quiet afternoon, made an important eightieth-minute save from Withers, who had got goal-side of the U's defence to run onto a pass from Saunders. Then came the disputed penalty award that allowed Colchester to keep in the thick of the promotion race. Three players were shown the yellow card – Smith and Elliott for the U's and Runcorn's Hagan.

Colchester: Barrett: Donald, Roberts, Cook, English, Elliott, Collins, Bennett (*sub* Kinsella 73), McDonough, McGavin, Smith. *Unused sub:* Grainger.
Runcorn: Palladino, Hughes, Redmond, Carroll, Hill, Hagan (*sub* Hawtin 64), Brabin, Harold, Shaughnessy, Saunders, Withers. *Unused sub:* Abrahams.

U'S PROVE TO BE A CLASS APART

Friday 18 October 1991　　　　　**Telford United 0 Colchester 3**
Referee: Mr T. Atkinson (Holywell)　　Attendance: 1,109

By Neal Manning, *East Anglian Daily Times*

Defeat in the final away match of last season against Telford United at the Bucks Head Ground went a long way towards preventing Colchester United from regaining their place in the Football League. But at the same venue last night, the U's found it all too easy against a Telford side that went down to their fifth successive defeat. Colchester's victory, however, was clearcut and comprehensive after they had established a 3-0 interval lead. Two more goals for player-coach Roy McDonough to take his tally to ten for the season paved the way for this latest success, with Nicky Smith adding a third with his second goal of the campaign. It was an efficient display by Colchester who, apart from the odd moment, were seldom troubled by a Telford side who started the evening just one place below them.

Not good enough

But the gap in class was evident, especially in the first half when Colchester established a winning lead. In the second period, the U's took their foot off the pedal and, in many ways, this was understandable. Telford, quite simply, were not good enough to give the U's many problems. McDonough, who gave way after taking a knock with quarter-of-an-hour left, had done his work in the first twenty-three minutes. It was early as the ninth minute that McDonough gave the U's the lead with a spectacular left-foot shot from the edge of the penalty area. Roberts knocked a free-kick up to McDonough who, with his back to goal, turned and let go with a strike that flew into the top corner of the net. After Myers had sent a free header wide of the upright, the U's increased their lead in the twenty-third minute with a penalty from McDonough. He had headed the ball through for McGavin, whose pace had taken away from the Telford defence. Inside the penalty area, Dyson flattened McGavin and, after the big defender had been booked, McDonough stepped up to score with a low right-foot shot into the bottom corner of the net. Colchester continued to look a cut above their opponents although, in the thirty-third minute, Barrett had to stretch to tip over a header from Nelson. Roberts was shown a yellow card after bringing Langford down in full flight before the U's scored again – and what a gift it was after a bad mistake by Humphries. The Telford full-back lost control of the ball midway inside his own half and Smith picked up, strode forward and beat Acton at his near post with a low shot. Cook, who had been suffering from a virus all week, was replaced by Kinsella in the sixty-second minute as the U's continued to keep charge, with Elliott having a fine match at the back. Bennett became the second U's player to be booked, in the seventy-second minute,

Nicky 'Smudger' Smith, scorer of his second goal of the season and United's third at Bucks Head, Telford.

for kicking the ball away before the fit-again Phillips replaced McDonough. Barrett excelled himself in the seventy-seventh minute by turning a Benbow shot on to the post while, at the other end, Acton denied McGavin with a full-length save. Victory was as easy as the scoreline suggests, and now the U's can take a break from league action with their FA Cup tie against Burton Albion in a week's time.

Telford: Acton, Humphries, Nelson, Dyson, Brindley (*sub* Worrall 45), Whittington, Myers, Grainger, Benbow, Langford, Parrish. *Unused sub:* Brown.
Colchester: Barrett, Donald, Roberts, Cook (*sub* Kinsella 62), English, Elliott, Collins, Bennett, McDonough (*sub* Phillips 75), McGavin, Smith.

COLCHESTER NEVER UNDER PRESSURE

Saturday 26 October 1991

Referee: Mr R.L. Bigger (Norfolk)

Colchester 5 Burton Albion 0
(FA Cup Fourth Qualifying Round)
Attendance: 2,547

By Neal Manning, *East Anglian Daily Times*

Colchester United duly booked their place in the first round proper of the FA Cup at Layer Road on Saturday but, apart from the final quarter-of-an-hour, their overall performance did not reach any great heights. Burton Albion, bottom of the Beazer Homes Premier Division, were never likely to cause an upset in the fourth qualifying round tie and they finally ran out of steam as the U's added three goals in the last ten minutes. 'Fitness told in the end, but the scoreline flattered us,' said Ian Phillips, who had his first full senior match of the season in place of cup-tied Paul Roberts. 'We were too comfortable, could have played better but were never really under any pressure.'

Tedious first-half

When United were awarded a penalty after just thirty-four seconds, most people expected the floodgates to open. That did not happen, however, and the fans had to suffer a tedious first half. When McGavin scored a quite spectacular goal in the fifty-first minute, it raised everybody's spirits in a tie in which the referee took six names, including those of McDonough and Collins, to push the U's pair a step closer to suspension. McDonough has now been booked four times and Collins three to take Colchester's overall total to sixteen for the season – not a record of which they will be particularly proud. Sensibly, McDonough withdrew both himself and Collins in the closing stages to avoid any possible further punishment.

McGavin the star

In many ways, Saturday's tie belonged to McGavin, who scored twice and was directly involved in the other three goals. McGavin's skills, when he really turned it on in the closing stages, destroyed a Burton side that was poor to say the least. The U's have never been beaten by a non-League side in an FA Cup tie at Layer Road, and that record was never under threat against Burton, who found themselves facing an uphill task after Bottomley had hauled down McGavin from behind in the first minute. McDonough stepped up to score his eleventh goal of the season. It was his fourth penalty in successive matches. Eventually, McGavin put a smile on the fans' faces with a goal that only he could have scored. Following a one-touch build-up, Bennett crossed from the right and McGavin, with his back to goal, found the net via the underside of the bar with a spectacular overhead kick. After that, the bookings continued and, by the sixty-seventh minute, four Burton players had been cautioned before youngsters Abrahams and Restarick replaced McDonough and Collins. McDonough's absence enabled McGavin to take his season's total to eight after Simms had brought him down in the penalty area in

Referee David Elleray lays the law down to Colchester boss Roy McDonough after the big striker had clashed with Burton Albion's Simon Redfearn. Colchester romped home by 5-0 in this FA Cup fourth qualifying round tie.

the eightieth minute. McGavin scored from the resultant kick with Goodwin getting his hands to the ball, but unable to prevent it from going into the net. Five minutes later, the combination of McGavin and Restarick produced a superb fourth goal. McGavin's close-controlled skills cut the Burton defence to ribbons to lay on a chance for Restarick. He scored his first senior goal with a well-taken rising shot into the roof of the net.

Goal tally of forty
Right on time, the U's completed a nap hand. McGavin burst down the left and, although Bennett just failed to reach his low cross, Kinsella was on hand to steer the ball into the net. The U's have now taken their goal tally to forty for the season in all competitions, and the day was completed with the news that Wycombe Wanderers had been beaten at Kidderminster in the Conference. It's back to league business for McDonough's men on Wednesday when they make the trip to Yeovil.

Colchester: Barrett, Donald, Phillips, Kinsella, English, Elliott, Collins (*sub* Restarick 77), Bennett, McDonough (*sub* Abrahams 74), McGavin, Smith.
Burton: Goodwin, Bottomley, Foster, Straw, Geelan, Simms, Davies, S. Redfern, Lycett, D. Redfern (*sub* Cordner 62), Hall (*sub* Sallis 53).

INJURY TIME WIN FOR COLCHESTER

Tuesday 30 October 1991
Referee: Mr R.E. Budden (Exeter)

Yeovil Town 0 Colchester 1
Attendance: 2,385

By Neal Manning, *East Anglian Daily Times*

Steve McGavin popped up in injury time at Huish Park last night to give Colchester United a priceless victory, but one they hardly deserved. A draw would have been the fairest outcome of a match that never reached any great heights, but McGavin's ninth goal of the season enabled the U's to leapfrog into second place behind Farnborough. It looked as though Colchester would draw a blank for the first time this season until McGavin's last-gasp winner. It was an untidy goal that decided the outcome with McGavin tapping the ball home from virtually on the goal line, after Smith's shot had rolled against the post. The goal was made possible in the first place when Man of the Match Roberts won the ball deep in his own half and set Donald on his way down the right. The full-back's cross-field pass was picked up by Smith, but Harrower got in a challenge before Smith got another touch and sent the ball rolling gently against the post. McGavin, who, like a lot of his colleagues, had had a quiet evening, was on hand to tap the ball into the empty net, much to the delight of the travelling fans. Yeovil, who have not won a Conference match since the end of August, looked there for the taking but the U's, after losing Bennett on the half-hour with a leg injury, were never able to stamp their authority on the match. Incidents were few and far between, with the U's creating fewer chances than they had done all season. Both goalkeepers were virtually unemployed but the U's defence, in which sweeper Roberts was outstanding, gave little away and, as a result, restricted Yeovil to few opportunities. The Somerset side, struggling near the foot of the table, had signed Andy Rowlands on loan from Torquay just four hours before the kick-off, and within eight minutes, he had headed wide from a Cooper cross. Four minutes later, Bennett flashed a left-foot shot against the bar after a corner had been knocked out, before Barrett had to make his only save of the match, turning behind a shot from Rowlands after twenty-four minutes. Goodwin replaced Bennett on the half-hour as the U's were forced to revert to an extra man in midfield, leaving just McDonough and McGavin up front. Yeovil did have the ball in the Colchester net after thirty-eight minutes when Rowlands fired home from close range, but it was disallowed for a foul by Spencer as he climbed for a cross from Carroll. The U's thought they might have had a penalty just before the interval, when McGavin was brought down following a defensive slip, but the referee was unimpressed. Smith fired into the side netting from an acute angle in the fifty-fifth minute before the U's went closest to breaking the deadlock in the sixty-third minute. McGavin was fouled on the edge of the penalty area and he curled a free-kick round the wall with his right foot and forced Fry to save just inside the far post. As the match wore on, the U's had to show their defensive qualities as Yeovil pressed forward, but then up popped McGavin to claim victory. If the U's go on to win the Conference title, then they might look back on last night's three points – two of them were certainly a bonus.

Two youngsters aimed to make an impression at Layer Road in 1991/92. Steve Restarick (above) notched his first senior goal in the FA Cup tie with Burton Albion, whilst big things are expected of tough-tackling left-back Martin Grainger (left).

Yeovil: Fry, Harrower, Rowbotham, Shail, Batty, Cooper, Carroll, Wallace, Rowlands, Spencer, Conning. *Unused subs:* McDermott and Wilson.

Colchester: Barrett, Donald, Roberts, Kinsella, English, Elliott, Collins, Bennett (*sub* Goodwin 30), McDonough, McGavin, Smith. *Unused sub:* Phillips.

BARRETT SPARES U'S BLUSHES

Saturday 2 November 1991
Referee: Mr G.T. Pearson
      (Kingston-Upon-Thames)

Colchester 2 Stafford Rangers 0
Attendance: 2,139

By Neal Manning, *East Anglian Daily Times*

Two moments of brilliance from Scott Barrett at Layer Road on Saturday prevented Colchester United from suffering severe embarrassment. For sixty-five minutes, Barrett, who went on to keep his fourth clean sheet, had been unemployed against struggling Stafford side that the U's should have sunk without trace long before the end. But then Barrett, surely the best goalkeeper outside the Football League, had to show his agility to deny Palgrave a goal and he followed it up five minutes from the end with an equally good save from Devlin. Two up at half-time, Colchester had the opportunity to run up a cricket score against Stafford, who were stripped of six first-team regulars for various reasons. Instead of rubbing in their superiority, they took their foot off the pedal, allowed Stafford a chink of daylight and, but for Barrett's two outstanding saves, the afternoon could have ended in real anti-climax. Barrett's first save from Palgrave's well-struck thirty-yard effort, after the full-back had been allowed to run unchallenged through the middle, was top class. Barrett reacted by pushing the ball into the air and then recovering at lightening speed to collect it at the second attempt.

Incredible save

Then Barrett produced an incredible save to deny Devlin, Stafford's highly-rated striker, after he had cashed in on a mistake by Kinsella. Devlin hit a ferocious shot from the edge of the penalty area, but Barrett's reflexes were more than equal to the shot. The U's performance, the second half in particular, earned them an ear-bashing from Ian Phillips. 'Very disappointing. In the end we have got to be pleased with the result. It could have two-two but for Barrett', he said. Nevertheless, Colchester extended their unbeaten run to ten matches and can now look forward to a battle royal at top-of-the-table Farnborough, who dropped two points as they were held to a goal-less draw by Yeovil. It was a pity that the U's were unable to produce their best form for an excellent gate of 2,139 considering the televised Rugby World Cup Final was obviously a big counter-attraction. As it was, they had to settle for two goals inside four minutes late in the first half. The first arrived in the thirty-fifth minute and provided Smith with his third goal of the campaign and his first at home. Following Bennett's cross from the right, McDonough headed the ball back into the goalmouth, where McGavin sent a header crashing against the bar. The rebound came out to Smith, who headed into the net with Price stranded out of position. It was another header that extended the U's lead and provided McDonough with his twelfth goal of the season. McGavin crossed from the left and McDonough, unmarked, stooped to head the ball inside the far post. After that, Colchester should have put the result beyond any reasonable doubt against a Stafford side packed full of youngsters that, at times, hung

Gary Bennett, scorer of a brace against Stafford, pictured in the fourth qualifying round FA Cup tie with Burton Albion.

on grimly. Lindsey, Devlin and substitute Bradshaw were all shown the yellow card for fouls, as U's promised so much but delivered so little. Last season, a 2-0 lead often proved precarious because of the failure to kill off the opposition when they had the chance. On Saturday there was a familiar ring, but fortunately Barrett came to the rescue when he was most needed. Although the U's have been somewhat disappointing in their past two games, they have still picked up maximum points and not conceded a goal. That, surely, is the hallmark of a team that goes on to win championships.

Colchester: Barrett, Donald (*sub* Goodwin 64), Roberts, Kinsella, English, Elliott, Collins, Bennett, McDonough (*sub* Restarick 74), McGavin, Smith.
Stafford: Price, Lindsey, Palgrave, Simpson, Wood, Berks, Wilson, Pope (*sub* Bradshaw 65), Tuohy, Newman, Devlin. *Unused sub:* Essex.

IMPRESSIVE U'S HIT THE TOP

Saturday 9 November 1991
Referee: Mr S. Tomlin (Lewes)

Farnborough Town 0 Colchester 2
Attendance: 3,069

By Neal Manning, *East Anglian Daily Times*

Colchester United proved a class apart as they went to the top of the GM Vauxhall Conference table for the first time this season on Saturday. Little Farnborough, who had been out in front for several weeks, were left to reflect that they were second best on their record-breaking day. More than 3,000 people packed into the Cherrywood Road ground – more than half of those coming from Essex – and the U's travelling fans were rewarded with a performance that was professional in the extreme. Five consecutive clean sheets is a tribute to the way that United have bolted the back door in recent weeks without losing any of their attacking instincts.

Better away

On a day when the Conference came very much under the spotlight, Farnborough boss Ted Pearce was honest with his assessment as he faced the biggest post-match press conference he has had to give in twenty-three years as manager of Farnborough. 'The scoreline was a true reflection of an excellent match. Colchester passed the ball better and had players that were more composed under pressure. In certain areas they were better than us and deserved their victory. I have told my players they can learn from some of the things Colchester did. We made two unpressurised errors and got punished for them,' he said.

Delayed kick-off

The kick-off had to be put back by a quarter-of-an-hour to allow the long queues to take their place in the ground, but, once the action started, the U's asserted their authority and it was only on the break that Farnborough posed any threat. What an important signing Paul Roberts has proved. His experience behind English and Elliott at the back has been one reason why Colchester now look far more solid than they did in the first few games of the season when they were punished for same bad mistakes – notably by Farnborough, who had inflicted upon them their only defeat to date. Roberts, however, did make one mistake, which might have proved costly. After he had lost possession midway inside the Farnborough half, the home side broke quickly and, with the U's defence stretched, Barrett came to the rescue with a fine close range save from Read. That was the closest Farnborough came to a goal, as the U's continued to impress with some good build-up from the back and midfield, but it took until midway through the second half to make their possession count.

Bennett scores

Appropriately, it was Bennett, on his 100th League appearance, who made the breakthrough in the sixty-seventh minute. McDonough, whose aerial ability was always a threat, flicked on a corner from Smith – one of thirteen that the U's earned in the match.

Shaun Elliott and the watching Tony English are just two of Colchester United's stalwart defence which conceded just 14 goals in the first 15 matches. United moved to the top of the GM Vauxhall Conference by virtue of a 2-0 win at deposed leaders Farnborough. It was a red letter day for Elliott as he scored his first goal for United with just ten minutes remaining.

After the Farnborough defence had failed to clear, Bennett struck with a low shot through a crowded goalmouth. The outcome, which never really looked in doubt even from the early stages, was finally confirmed when Elliott scored his first goal for the club in the eightieth minute. Three minutes earlier, Elliott had shot against a post from a Smith corner on the right before heading home unchallenged from Collins' flag-kick from the other side of the pitch. Elliott's first goal means that only Donald and Roberts in the U's full-strength line-up have not scored to date. This proves they are not reliant or goals from just one section of the side. Bookings for McGavin and Elliott were two more Colchester could have done without. Nevertheless, McDonough was more than happy. 'A great result and a good team performance. We were a bit leggy and are normally sharper than that. But it sets us up nicely for Saturday's FA Cup tie against Exeter.' In his programme notes, Ted Pearce had castigated the apathetic support for his team. How he must have envied the huge following that the U's enjoyed on a day when Conference football was given a further boost. Even Graham Kelly (the FA's chief executive), who was a guest of Farnborough, could not fail to have been impressed.

Farnborough: Thompson, Stemp, Baker, Broome (*sub* Rogers 80), Bye, Wigmore (*sub* Fleming 82), Hobson, Doherty, Horton, Read, Holmes.
Colchester: Barrett, Donald, Roberts, Kinsella, English, Elliott, Collins, Bennett (*sub* Cook 74), McDonough (*sub* Restarick 85), McGavin, Smith.

GARY BENNETT'S MISSES COSTLY FOR COLCHESTER

Saturday 16 November 1991

Referee: Mr G.A. Pooley
(Bishop's Stortford)

Colchester 0 Exeter City 0
(FA Cup First Round)
Attendance: 4,965

By Neal Manning, *East Anglian Daily Times*

Gary Bennett was left to reflect on now he failed to convert even one of the four clearcut chances that came his way in Saturday's thrilling FA Cup first round tie against Exeter City at Layer Road. There would be no need for a replay on Wednesday week if Bennett's finishing, which has already brought him eight goals this season, had been up to scratch. On top of that, Steve McGavin, who again attracted scouts from First and Second Division clubs, was guilty of missing a gilt-edged opportunity as the Conference leaders failed to turn their supremacy into goals. Exeter had to play for all but the first eighteen minutes with ten men after their assistant manager, Steve Williams, had been sent off for a second bookable offence.

Some consolation

The Third Division side was delighted to escape with a draw in a tie that lived up to its pre-match billing. 'Football was the winner,' said U's captain Tony English, finding some consolation for his side not making sure of a second round place. The draw is today. The near 5,000 crowd could not complain about the entertainment that was on offer or the way Colchester served up some slick soccer using the full width of the pitch. 'The football we played in the second half was the best we have produced this season,' said a disappointed U's player-coach, Roy McDonough. 'But if you can't take your chance from six yards, you don't deserve to win.' In addition to the glaring miss, a goal-line clearance and the width of the crossbar came to Exeter's rescue. It was all the more frustrating because the U's demonstrated on this big occasion what a good side they are. No one could fail to have been impressed with their general play in an excellent all-round team performance. Even Alan Ball, the Exeter manager, admitted, 'Colchester can count themselves unlucky. They played some super stuff and I am just happy to have the chance of another crack at them. But if our home advantage doesn't pay off in the replay, I'll be disappointed.' The performance of Mark Kinsella was one of the highlights of the afternoon. Playing in the sweeper's role in place of the cup-tied Paul Roberts, the highly-rated young Irishman demonstrated what a big future he could have in the game. 'Mark was different class,' enthused Ian Phillips. 'He's got a good football brain and he was the best player on the pitch by a mile. Kinsella has not played as a sweeper since last season in the youth team, but he read the game like a book, displaying his all-round talents to the full.' Although there were five bookings – including one for Colchester's Donald – and a sending-off, it was not a dirty match by any stretch of the imagination. Competitive, yes,

Exeter City defender Andy Cook clears the ball from the grounded striker Roy McDonough with Warren Donald (left) looking on.

and the will to win was clear for everyone to see. It is, of course, hypothetical what effect Williams' dismissal had on the tie. After his departure, Exeter had to re-group, but apart from the odd moment of danger on the break, they were forced to defend in depth.

Struck the bar

There were times towards the end when the U's laid siege to the Exeter goal, but the ball would not go in. Bennett, who struck the bar from substitute Grainger's cross in the eighty-first minute, should have had the tie wrapped up before then. His first miss came as early as the ninth minute, after the immaculate Kinsella had played the ball over the top of the Exeter defence for Bennett to run on to, but he mis-kicked wide. It was in the second half that the chances went begging, with Bennett, in particular, and McGavin the culprits. It was the first time this season the U's had failed to score in a match, ironically on the day when they had created the most clearcut chances.

Colchester: Barrett, Donald, J. Cook, Kinsella, English, Elliott, Collins, Bennett, McDonough, McGavin, Smith (*sub* Grainger 73). *Unused sub:* Restarick.
Exeter: Miller, Hiley, A. Cook, Williams, Daniels, Whiston, Hilaire, Brown, Moran, Chapman, Kelly. *Unused subs:* Dolan, Redwood.

U'S SPARKLE – AT A COST

Saturday 23 November 1991
Referee: Mr D. Orr (Iver, Bucks)

Colchester 3 Welling United 1
Attendance: 2,933

By Neal Manning, *East Anglian Daily Times*

Colchester United stretched their unbeaten run to thirteen matches with a sparkling second-half performance at Layer Road on Saturday, but victory was gained at a cost. Shaun Elliott tore a calf muscle before the interval and is almost certainly out of Wednesday's FA Cup first round replay at Exeter. And with Paul Roberts cup-tied, United will be without two key defenders. The U's hopes of setting a new club record of seven consecutive clean sheets were dashed when a mistake by Mark Kinsella allowed Welling to score in the sixty-second minute. It was the first goal that Scott Barrett had conceded in well over 609 minutes of football, but the important thing was that Colchester scored three more goals to take their GM Vauxhall Conference League total to thirty-nine and maintain their top-of-the-table position.

Hardly recognisable

After the euphoria of the Exeter cup tie seven days earlier, the U's were hardly recognisable during a very disappointing first half in which they failed to create a single clearcut opportunity. Welling, in fact, missed a good chance to go in front in the thirty-ninth minute when Abbott shot straight at Barrett from close range. Some straight talking during the half-time interval obviously had the desired effect. The U's, with Cook on in place of the injured Elliott and Kinsella dropping back to sweeper, came out with all guns blazing. Within six minutes they had broken the deadlock with a fine goal from Gary Bennett, before substitute Cook increased the lead with a spectacular thirty-yard strike on the hour. Welling reduced the arrears before skipper Tony English scored his second goal of the season in the seventy-third minute from the fifteenth corner of the match, most of which had come during a dominant second period. On the debit side, however, the U's picked up two more bookings with Roy McDonough, who had his most subdued match of the season, earning a fifth caution, which edges him nearer suspension. Donald was shown the yellow card for the second successive match, while three Welling players – Clemmence, Brown and Reynolds – all suffered the same fate. The first half was certainly best forgotten, but the crowd, which failed to top the 3,000 mark, were treated to an exhilarating second period. Bennett, who missed four good chances against Exeter, made amends with a very good opener. Running onto a Kinsella pass over the top of the Welling defence, Bennett controlled the bouncing ball well before scoring his ninth goal of the season with a low shot past the advancing Baron. Nine minutes later, Cook scored his first goal for the club with a magnificent effort that had the crowd off their seats. After Collins' corner had only been half-cleared, Cook let go with a right-foot shot from all of thirty yards that never deviated in flight and flew into the roof of the net. A mistake by Kinsella two minutes later gave Welling some hope. Trying to be over elaborate as he brought the

Midfield signing Jason Cook shows just why Roy McDonough brought him in from neighbours Southend United. Tenacious in the tackle, Cook also possesses a lethal strike.

ball out of his own penalty area, the young Irishman passed straight to Abbott. He, in turn, picked out the unmarked Robbins, who beat the exposed Barrett from close range with ease. All was well, however, in the seventy-third minute when English popped up with his second goal of the season. Following Smith's corner on the right, Bennett crossed into the penalty area where the U's captain flung himself full length to head a picture goal. Bennett had the ball in the Welling net again four minutes from time, but it was disallowed because of an earlier infringement. So, it all came good for the U's in the end, but they will be hoping that Saturday's second-half performance will be repeated for the whole of Wednesday's FA Cup replay at Exeter.

Colchester: Barrett, Donald, Roberts, Kinsella, English, Elliott (*sub* Cook 45), Collins, Bennett, McDonough, McGavin, Smith. *Unused sub:* Restarick.
Welling: Baron, Hone, Clemmence, Brown, Ransom, Berry, White, Francis, Abbott, Robbins, Reynolds (*sub* Robinson 54). *Unused sub:* Burgess.

NOW COLCHESTER PAY THE PENALTY

Wednesday 27 November 1991

Exeter City 0 Colchester 0
(FA Cup First Round Replay)
[Exeter won 4-2 on penalties, after extra time]

Referee: Mr G. Pooley
      (Bishop's Stortford)

Attendance: 4,666

By Neal Manning, *East Anglian Daily Times*

Colchester United went out of the FA Cup at St James' Park last night – beaten in a penalty shoot-out by Third Division side Exeter City. Kevin Miller, the Exeter goalkeeper, emerged as the hero of the night, first by saving spot-kicks from Nicky Smith and Mark Kinsella, and then stepping up to beat his opposite number, Scott Barrett, to guide his side through to the second round by a 4-2 margin in the penalty decider. Miller had made an even more important contribution in the first minute of injury time with a brilliant save from Warren Donald that took this first round replay into extra time. After a goal-less first match at Layer Road eleven days ago, it was a repeat last night and, by the end of extra time, neither side had managed to break the deadlock after 210 minutes of endeavour. So it was down to the unsatisfactory business of deciding the outcome from the penalty spot, and Exeter held their nerve at the vital time. Roy McDonough scored with the first spot-kick and Gary Chapman levelled. Then Miller pushed away Smith's kick before Williams gave Exeter the advantage by scoring from his effort.

Squared

Martin Grainger squared the matter before Andy Cook regained Exeter's lead. Then Miller saved again, this time from Kinsella, and it was left to Miller to drive home his kick to send Exeter through to the next round and a home tie with Swansea. It was heartbreaking for the U's to go out of the competition in this way, but that is now the name of the game with FA Cup replays. There had been nothing to choose between the sides in the 210 minutes that had preceded the penalty shoot-out. Chances were few and far between until the closing stages when ten-man Exeter (a player short after Kelly had been carried off with a knee injury on seventy-four minutes, shortly after making a double substitution) left few gaps. The U's started the match with McDonough at the back in place of the injured Elliott and, in the first period, they soaked up everything that Exeter had to offer. By half-time, Barrett had been forced to save on only one occasion. Kinsella was again excellent in his sweeper's role but there was not a great deal for the crowd to enthuse about.

Late challenge

Hilaire was booked for a late challenge on McDonough in the fifty-first minute and gradually Colchester began to put their game together, but their final ball into the penalty area could have been better. Marshall, a late replacement for the injured Moran, forced

Colchester player-manager Roy McDonough in a tussle with Exeter City goalkeeper Kevin Miller in the first clash at Layer Road. Miller had the last laugh as his side won through on penalties, despite United not conceding a goal in 240 minutes of open play.

Barrett into a diving save in the sixty-second minute before both sides made substitutions. Goodwin, who had run out of steam, was replaced by Grainger in the sixty-fifth minute and, a minute later, Exeter sent on Redwood and Cole in place of Wimbleton and Hilaire. McDonough went up front to bring the U's strike-force up to its normal three before Exeter lost Kelly with strained knee ligaments. With the tie heading for extra time, both sides (especially the U's) came close to grabbing what would have been the all-important goal. Collins hooked the ball off the line in the eighty-eighth minute after Whiston had flicked on a corner from Williams and then Donald, in the first minute of injury time, brought the best out of Miller with a snap-shot from the edge of the penalty area. The Exeter 'keeper responded by taking off and turning the ball over the bar.

Diving save

At the other end, Marshall produced a fine diving save from Barrett's twenty-five-yard shot before the match moved into extra time. Bennett just failed to get his head to a Smith cross in the ninety-fifth minute, while Chapman flashed a shot just wide in the second period of extra time. The U's just missed out on gaining a small piece of FA Cup history – Scunthorpe became the first team ever to go out of the competition on penalties when they lost to Rotherham on Tuesday night. But Colchester became the unlucky second team to do so.

Exeter: Miller, Brown, A. Cook, Williams, Daniels, Whiston, Hilaire
(*sub* Redwood 66), Wimbleton (*sub* Cole 66), Marshall, Kelly, Chapman.
Colchester: Barrett, Donald, J. Cook, Kinsella, English, Goodwin (*sub* Grainger
65), Collins, Bennett (*sub* Restarick 109), McDonough, McGavin.

McDONOUGH UPSET WITH REFEREE

Saturday 30 November 1991
Referee: Mr J. McGrath (Birkenhead)

Northwich Victoria 1 Colchester 1
Attendance: 1,042

By Neal Manning, *East Anglian Daily Times*

It all happened for Roy McDonough as his Colchester United side, hit by injury and illness, maintained their unbeaten Conference away record in the drab setting of the Drill Field on Saturday. A first-half booking means that McDonough now faces suspension, but his seventy-fifth minute equaliser gave the U's a point and, with closest rivals Wycombe being surprisingly held at home by Cheltenham, the Manager of the Month award for November must be on its way. While satisfied with a point against Northwich Victoria in the circumstances, McDonough finished his day by having a blast at the referee, whom he felt had been hard on his team. The U's player-coach, who did not know what his line-up would be until just before the kick-off because of a stomach bug that had struck many of his players, said: 'Officials can cost you your living with their decisions. The penalty he gave against Paul Roberts was a joke. Their player was only two yards away when he hit his shot and it caught 'Robbo' under the armpit. We should have had a penalty earlier on when Eamonn Collins was pushed as he went for my flick-on, but the referee didn't want to know.' McDonough's other big gripe about the Conference is the standard of refereeing, but as far as Saturday's match was concerned, a draw was perhaps a fair reflection. It took an hour for the U's to really get going. Their first effort on goal did not come until that time, and they only won one corner throughout the match.

Self-destruction

True, they finished the stronger side and looked more likely to go on to win after McDonough's equaliser but in the first half they could have been punished more heavily as they pushed the self-destruction button. Two badly misplaced back passes, first by Smith in the thirty-eighth minute and then by McDonough four minutes later, were fortunate to go unpunished. Smith's attempted back pass from on the touchline was intercepted by Stringer, who rounded the advancing Barrett, but his shot lacked pace and Donald got across to clear. McDonough's mistake was even worse, as he passed straight back to O'Connor. Fortunately, Barrett anticipated the situation, advanced quickly and then made a fine point-blank save from Northwich's leading scorer. The U's got off the hook on those two occasions, but they were incensed a minute before half-time when the referee awarded the penalty that was harsh in the extreme. Butler, however, made no mistake with the resultant spot kick.

English injury

In the first three months of the season, Colchester have had to make few changes, but the stomach bug that struck with a vengeance and English's hamstring injury (which is likely to keep him out for another fortnight) caught them on the hop. Bennett and English did not make the starting line-up; Smith played for fifty-eight minutes feeling far from well – even

50

Following an impressive nine-goal haul since the start of the season Steve McGavin, shown in action against Bath City in August, endured a blank November.

Kinsella was only a substitute because there was nobody else – while Elliott, not fully recovered from a calf injury, had to play and excelled at the heart of the defence alongside stand-in captain Roberts. Phillips took over the sweeper's role with Roberts moving forward. In the second half, the U's, who had lacked the necessary determination in some areas in the first period, showed up much better. Smith, unable to do his normal work up and down the left because he felt too weak, gave way to Kinsella after fifty-eight minutes.

First on target

Grainger, who played in midfield, got in Colchester's first on-target effort on the hour before the equaliser arrived, following a quickly taken free-kick by McGavin. Collins, who had now begun to impose himself, swept the ball out to Grainger, whose cross was flicked on by McGavin to the far post, where McDonough bundled it in from close range. McDonough almost snatched a late winner with a header that flashed just wide of the near post. Now the U's, who should have a full squad available apart from English, will be hoping to open up a three-point gap at the top when they travel to Stafford tomorrow night.

Northwich Victoria: Bullock, Locke, Butler, Jones, Hancock, Stringer, Ainsworth, Feeley, Easter, O'Connor (*sub* Graham 82), Blain. *Unused sub:* Hemmings.
Colchester: Barrett, Donald, Roberts, Grainger, Phillips, Elliott, Collins, Cook, McDonough, McGavin, Smith (*sub* Kinsella 58). *Unused sub:* Restarick.

INJURED ENGLISH MISSED BY U'S

Tuesday 3 December 1991
Referee: Mr R.H. Andrews
(Warrington)

Stafford Rangers 3 Colchester 3
Attendance: 961

By Neal Manning, *East Anglian Daily Times*

Colchester United held the lead three times against lowly Stafford Rangers at Marston Road last night, but had to settle for a draw in the end. Although they stretched their unbeaten Conference run to twelve matches, the U's will be disappointed not to have taken maximum points and increased their lead at the top to three points. After establishing a one-goal lead at the interval, it all happened in a fast and furious second half in which there were five goals in under half-an-hour and, but for a fine save from Scott Barrett two minutes from the end, Colchester could have suffered defeat.

Whirlwind start
In the second period, the U's never looked comfortable in defence as eager Stafford hit them hard and, at times, made them look decidedly ragged. The absence of skipper Tony English was a big blow and the reshuffled defence never coped comfortably. Stafford made a whirlwind start, but the U's coped well enough, although Kinsella picked up his first booking of the season for a foul on the lively Devlin. Gradually, the U's began to stamp their authority and class on the match, and it was no surprise when they took the lead in the forty-first minute, with Gary Bennett's tenth goal of the season and the club's 50th in all competitions. At one end, Barrett had made a fine save from an angled shot from Hope, and the U's immediately broke away with Collins finding Bennett, and he raced through before tucking a right-foot shot from the edge of the penalty area beyond the diving Price's right hand. But the U's failed to capitalise on that lead, although Cook went close three minutes into the second half with a shot on the turn that hit the underside of the bar. Stafford equalised in the fifty-ninth minute when Wolverson took a pass from Hemming in his stride before firing a right-foot shot into the bottom corner of the net. It was the first goal that Colchester had conceded against Stafford in four matches. All looked well when McGavin scored his first goal since the end of October to regain the lead for the U's. Collins' free-kick from just outside the penalty area went wide to Bennett and from his low cross into the goal-mouth, McGavin comfortably side-footed home for his eleventh goal of the season.

Low shot
But within two minutes, Stafford were back on terms after McDonough, helping back in defence from a free-kick, brought down Hemming as he turned in the penalty area. Simpson made no mistake from the resultant spot-kick. A bad mistake by Pearson in the seventy-seventh minute enabled Colchester to take the lead for the third time. His attempted back header fell into the path of Bennett, and he scored his second goal of the

Seemingly surrounded by Runcorn players in an earlier fixture, Shaun Elliott and his fellow defenders threw away the lead three times at Stafford Rangers as the lowly hosts secured an unexpected 3-3 draw.

match, slipping the ball past the advancing Price. A mistake at the other end, however, lead to Stafford becoming the first team this season to score three goals against Colchester on their travels. A slip by Roberts let in Bradshaw and he strode through before driving a low shot under Barrett's body. Then Barrett came to the rescue to deny Stafford what would have been a dramatic winner in this topsy-turvy affair. The U's defensive performance will have provided food for thought for watching Wycombe manager Martin O'Neill before Saturday's top-of-the-table clash at Layer Road. There is every hope that English will be able to return following his hamstring injury. On the evidence of last night, he will be badly needed.

Stafford: Price, Pearson, Bradshaw, Simpson, Essex, Wood, Wolverson, Hemming, Hope, Berks, Devlin. *Unused subs:* Baker and Newman.
Colchester: Barrett. Donald, Roberts, Kinsella, Cook, Elliott, Collins, Bennett, McDonough, McGavin, Smith. *Unused subs:* Grainger and Restarick.

McGAVIN STRIKES FORM AT THE RIGHT TIME

Saturday 7 December 1991   **Colchester 3 Wycombe Wanderers 0**
Referee: Mr P. Taylor (Cheshunt)   Attendance: 5,053

By Neal Manning, *East Anglian Daily Times*

Steve McGavin could not have picked a better moment to regain his scoring touch with two second-half goals before the biggest crowd of the season at Layer Road on Saturday. McGavin took his total to thirteen and became joint leading scorer alongside Roy McDonough, with Gary Bennett, who opened the scoring against Wycombe Wanderers, just one behind his fellow strikers. The U's strike-force has produced thirty-eight of the fifty-five goals scored so far, and that's just one reason why they have now opened up a four-point lead at the top of the GM Vauxhall Conference after completing their second double of the season over their closest rivals.

Showed quality

Before his goal in the 3-3 draw at Stafford in midweek, McGavin had gone six matches without finding the net, but he showed his quality as the U's overpowered and outclassed Wycombe with an impressive second-half performance that had the hallmark of champions. Martin O'Neill, an admirer of McGavin, locked his team in the dressing room after watching them cave in to a U's side – again without the injured English – who, in the end, were well worth their emphatic victory. True, they were helped by some poor goalkeeping by Hyde, who could be blamed for two of the goals, but overall Colchester again showed that they are without doubt the best team in the Conference. The U's amply demonstrated their strength. While the strikers took the honours for scoring the goals, it was at the back and in midfield where the decisive battles were won. Kinsella again impressed the watching scouts with another fine performance, this time in the central defensive role alongside the outstanding Elliott. Roberts returned to sweeper, which is undoubtedly his best position. Donald, so consistent this season, curbed the threat of Wycombe's potential danger man Guppy to such an extent that he was withdrawn midway through the second half.

No real threat

In the first period, the U's never really got going in the way they know they can, with Wycombe having the better of the exchanges as they closed the home side down quickly. However, apart from the odd moment, they never proved a real threat and Barrett only had one save to make throughout. It was slightly against the run of play when Bennett scored his twelfth goal of the season in the thirty-third minute, helped by a bad mistake from Hyde. After Smith had knocked the ball forward, Cook released Bennett as he made a darting run through the heart of the defence. Bennett hit a low show that caught the heel of Crossley, but the ball did not deviate and it was a surprise to everyone when it squirmed under the body of the diving Hyde. After that, Hyde, who allowed Barrett's long

Colchester v. Wycombe Wanderers

Colchester United's Gary Bennett (8) is congratulated by player-manager Roy McDonough after putting his side ahead with a deflected shot after thirty-three minutes of top-of-the-table match against Wycombe Wanderers at Layer Road.

clearance to bounce over his head for the U's winner at Wycombe in September, was a bag of nerves. It was another Barrett clearance that set up the second goal in the sixty-second minute.

Outstretched arms

The ball bounced over McDonough to McGavin, who had cut in from the right before bending a left-foot shot that went in off the inside of the far post. It was a quality goal from a quality player. McGavin completed the scoring four minutes from time. After Hyde had made a fine save from him, McGavin collected Smith's throw-in on the left and beat the Wycombe 'keeper with a cross-shot that went over his outstretched arms as he dived at full length. The U's extended their unbeaten Conference run to fourteen matches – dating back to early September – and this latest victory sets them up nicely for the heavy holiday programme, which is just around the corner. Next Saturday, Colchester head north to Gateshead and will, after all, have McDonough free to play if he chooses. His sixth booking of the season at Northwich ten days ago was worth only two points, which leaves him just short of the suspension mark.

Colchester: Barrett, Donald, Roberts, Kinsella, Cook, Elliott, Collins, Bennett, McDonough, McGavin, N. Smith. *Unused subs:* Grainger and Restarick.
Wycombe: Hyde, Cousins (*sub* Cooper 51), Stapleton, Crossley, Creaser, G. Smith, Hutchinson, Carroll, West, Scott, Guppy (*sub* Deakin 71).

COLCHESTER SEVEN POINTS CLEAR

Saturday 14 December 1991
Referee: Mr G. Bradbury (York)

Gateshead 0 Colchester 2
Attendance: 542

From the *East Anglian Daily Times*

Colchester United established a seven-point lead over Wycombe at the top of the GM Vauxhall Conference, although they have now played two matches more than their Buckinghamshire rivals. While Roy McDonough's U's were capturing the points from struggling Gateshead on Saturday, Wycombe's home match with Northwich Victoria was frosted off. The weather in the North-East has been far less severe than in East Anglia, and conditions at the International Stadium were not too bad. The match started at 1.30 p.m. because Gateshead's floodlights are currently being repaired and the referee wanted to ensure that the action finished in daylight.

Key men missing
Colchester, missing influential men Tony English at the back and Steve McGavin up front, made just the start that McDonough wanted. The match was only five minutes old when Gary Bennett netted with a crisp volley from six yards, after Restarick had outpaced former Southampton defender Gerry Forrest down the left. On the half-hour, Colchester scored their second, which relieved them of a great deal of pressure. Bennett provided the cross and McDonough rose to net his fourteenth goal of the season. It was a powerful header and gave goalkeeper Smith no chance.

Barrett shines
From then on, Colchester perhaps relaxed a bit. Certainly Gateshead, now managed by former Northern Ireland international Tommy Cassidy, came back into the match. A minute before the break, Steve Chambers was denied by the woodwork. Later, Gateshead did enough in attack to allow Scott Barrett to underline the claim that he is the best goalkeeper in non-League football. Barrett made a fingertip save to turn away a header from Nigel Saddington in the fifty-second minute and saved well from Steve Lamb, the former Hartlepool striker, in the seventy-second minute.

Break football
Colchester, with the buffer of a two-goal lead, were prepared to play break football, which almost brought them two further goals in the closing stages. Eamonn Collins hit the underside of the bar with a curling free-kick, which the referee ruled had not crossed the line, and McDonough rattled the woodwork with a powerful header in the eighty-third minute. United are now unbeaten in fourteen matches, and they are certainly well placed for a return to the Fourth Division of the Barclays League after a couple of seasons in the wilderness. Gateshead were themselves founder members of the Football League when their home was at Redheugh Park, but now they are battling to keep their Conference

56

Gateshead's impressive 12,000-seater International Stadium scoreboard spells out a welcome message for Colchester United. However, only 542 watch from the main stand.

status. Only 542 turned up to watch the Conference leaders in action, hardly a figure to pay the wages, but it was another chance for the U's to show that they are a cut above the Conference, and they took the opportunity with both hands.

Gateshead: Smith, Forrest, Saddington, Lowery, Corner, Halliday, Chambers, Bell, Farrey, Lamb, Veart (*sub* Dixon 66). *Unused sub:* Johnson.
Colchester: Barrett, Donald, Roberts, Kinsella, Cook, Elliott, Collins, Bennett, McDonough, Restarick (*sub* Abrahams 84), Smith. *Unused sub:* Grainger.

WEAKENED U'S HIT FOR SIX IN THE FOG

Monday 16 December 1991

Referee: Mr J.F. Moore (Norwich)

Colchester 2 Wycombe Wanderers 6
(Bob Lord Trophy Second Round)
Attendance: 919

By Neal Manning, *East Anglian Daily Times*

Colchester United went out of the Bob Lord Trophy at a foggy Layer Road last night but they won't be shedding too many tears about that. Wycombe sent their full-strength side, determined to avenge the two league defeats they have suffered at the hands of the U's, and went away with a convincing 6-2 victory. That means that Wycombe now face a two-legged semi-final, something that Colchester did not want. With a return to the Football League their main priority, this competition might have proved to be an inconvenience had they won last night. With fog making it impossible to see the far side of the pitch, it was often difficult to follow the play, but the main thing was that the game was completed and it provided eight goals into the bargain.

Full run-out

The U's started the match without five first-team regulars, but it gave the opportunity for youngsters like Partner and Restarick to have a full run-out. Colchester's captain, English, out for the last four first-team matches with a hamstring injury, made a welcome return. He came through the tie without any apparent reaction and will be in line for a place against Witton on Saturday. The U's strength was further reduced in the sixty-first minute when Roberts limped off with a leg injury, and McDonough decided to withdraw himself to give Gray an opportunity. Colchester started with McDonough in the sweeper's role and Roberts in midfield, and were on level terms at a goal apiece by the interval.

Convincing winner

But Wycombe cruised to victory in the second half with the fog getting thicker, and they ran out convincing winners in the end. Smith, a former Colchester player, was booked as early as the second minute when he clattered into Roberts. Wycombe drew first blood in the twenty-seventh minute; Hutchinson, after combining with Carroll on the right, crossed and West headed beyond Barrett. The U's equalised in the thirty-fourth minute following a well-worked move, initially involving Roberts and McGavin. McGavin, who missed Saturday's Conference match at Gateshead, crossed from the right to the far post, Abrahams hooked into the goalmouth, and Restarick provided the finishing touch. The second half was only six minutes old when Wycombe regained the lead with a goal that few people were able to see because of the fog. It transpired that following a corner from the right by Guppy, Scott headed in at the near post. Hannigan replaced Roberts in the fifty-fifth minute and, four minutes after his arrival, he forced a brilliant save from Hyde, the Wycombe goalkeeper, who was jeered every time he touched the ball. It was only ten days previously that Hyde had been responsible for two of the U's goals in the vital top-

Gary Bennett evades a Wycombe tackle watched closely by Warren Donald, Paul Roberts and match referee Paul Taylor in the earlier GM Vauxhall Conference clash at Layer Road.

of-the-table Conference match, but on this occasion he produced a breathtaking save from Hannigan's twenty-five-yard drive, turning the ball onto the bar at full stretch.

Further behind

The U's fell further behind in the sixty-first minute when Hutchinson scored from Guppy's cross and, four minutes later, the same player cut in from the right before scoring from the edge of the area. Creaser headed home a Guppy free-kick in the seventy-sixth minute to make it five, before McGavin cut the arrears four minutes from time with a superb solo goal. McGavin beat three men in the penalty area before sending a rising shot into the roof of the net. There was still time for Wycombe to score again though, with West heading home substitute Cooper's cross in the last minute. Mike Masters, the American striker who spent six months on loan at Layer Road last season, returned to the club yesterday and starts training today. Ian Phillips, however, is likely to be out for the next six weeks. He goes into hospital on Friday for an operation on a torn calf muscle.

Colchester: Barrett, Cook, Grainger, Partner, Roberts (*sub* Hannigan 55), English, Goodwin, Restarick, McDonough (*sub* Gray 61), McGavin, Abrahams.
Wycombe: Hyde, Cousins (*sub* Cooper 70), Stapleton, Crossley, Creaser, Smith, Hutchinson, Carroll, West, Scott (*sub* Deakin 70), Guppy.

'SUPER SUB' ENGLISH RESCUES COLCHESTER

Saturday 21 December 1991   Colchester 3 Witton Albion 2
Referee: Mr C.T. Finch (Elmswell)   Attendance: 2,842

By Neal Manning, *East Anglian Daily Times*

When Colchester United went two goals up in the first nine minutes at Layer Road on Saturday, Witton Albion manager Peter O'Brien thought he would need a calculator to keep score. It looked as though the floodgates would open as the U's exposed the limitations in the visitors' defence. O'Brien said: 'I thought a cricket scoreboard would be needed to keep pace with the goals Colchester were going to put past us. For the first half-hour, we were at sixes and sevens and we defended like a Sunday morning side.' With Colchester playing like a top-of-the-table side against the strong wind, Witton were never in it, but when the impressive Thomas pulled a goal back just before half-time, the picture began to change.

Chances squandered
Within a minute of the start of the second half, Thomas had scored again to give Witton a chance of winning their first Conference match for more than two months. Even with the wind at their backs, the U's were unimpressive, yet they squandered enough chances before 'super sub' Tony English came to the rescue with his seventy-ninth-minute winner. The fit-again English, who had come off the bench only fourteen minutes earlier, headed home Smith's corner at the far the post. By the end, the U's were grateful for the victory that keeps them seven points clear of Wycombe at the top.

Flattering result
Although Witton, who caused Colchester problems on the break in the second half, came close to taking something from the match, O'Brien said the result flattered his team. 'I'm not going to kid myself. We had a bit of luck because Colchester missed chances galore. We could easily have been 4-0 down after half-an-hour and in the second half they missed some chances they would normally have taken.' Ian Phillips, who must have been as frustrated as the crowd during the second half, said: 'In the first half-hour, we were different class. The wind didn't help, but you won't see a better goal than Thomas' first for Witton.' On the last Saturday before Christmas, when crowds are normally at their lowest, the gate of 2,842 was very good indeed. And the U's fans did not have to wait long for something to shout about.

McGavin's opener
Within three minutes, McGavin had fired them in front, scoring from close range after McDonough had flicked on a corner from Smith. Six minutes later, and the U's reached a landmark with their fiftieth Conference goal of the season, scored by Bennett who became joint leading scorer with McGavin at fourteen apiece, one more than McDonough.

Gary Bennett, centre, takes on the Witton defence during a period of sustained United pressure in U's 3-2 win at Layer Road.

McGavin and McDonough combined to set up Bennett, whose shot was saved by Mason. The Witton goalkeeper was unable to hold the ball and Bennett made no mistake when the rebound came back to him. Three minutes before the interval, the U's were shocked when Thomas reduced the arrears. Kinsella was caught in possession out on the touchline by Thomas, who cut in and then deliberately curled the ball, with the help of the wind, over Barrett and into the net via the inside of the far post.

Blown by wind

Witton equalised when Thomas volleyed the ball into the roof of the net, after McCluskie had headed on at the near post. Barrett, however, was adamant that the ball had gone behind and was blown back into play by the wind. After that, Witton had a couple of chances to have further embarrassed the U's, but all was well when English popped up with the winner.

Colchester: Barrett, Donald, Roberts, Kinsella (*sub* English 65), Cook, Elliott, Collins, Bennett (*sub* Restarick 78), McDonough, McGavin, Smith.
Witton: Mason, Cuddy, Coathup, McNeilis, Morgan, Anderson, Thomas, Wilson (*sub* Jim Connor 84), McCluskie, Stewart (*sub* Alford 82), Joe Connor.

WALSH STRIKES TO END RUN

Thursday 26 December 1991
Referee: Mr J. Smyth (Sussex)

Redbridge Forest 2 Colchester 1
Attendance: 2,327

By Neal Manning, *East Anglian Daily Times*

Mario Walsh, jeered by Colchester United's travelling fans just about every time he touched the ball, had the last laugh in the Boxing Day sunshine at Victoria Road yesterday morning. Walsh, sold to Redbridge Forest at the end of October for £15,000, popped up with an eighty-first-minute winner that handed Colchester their first away defeat of the season and also ended an unbeaten Conference run of fifteen matches. The irony was certainly not lost on Walsh, who said: 'It was nice to score against Colchester. You could not have written the script any better.'

Early boost

Despite being given an early boost by Roy McDonough's third-minute goal, the U's, who left out Collins for the first time this season, did not capitalise on their lead in a scrappy match which was spoiled by some of the officials' decisions. Redbridge have now won nine of their last ten matches and manager John Still, who has transformed them in the last couple of months, said: 'It was a typical Christmas game, with not a lot of football played. There wasn't much to choose between the sides, but Walsh took his chance at a time when Colchester were having the better of the exchanges.' It was only in the first quarter-of-an-hour and in the last few minutes before half-time that the U's showed their pedigree. With wind advantage in the second half, they failed to use the width of the pitch and continually thumped the ball forward in the hope that something would happen. Redbridge goalkeeper, Ian Bennett, did not have to make a save throughout, despite the fact that the U's had far more possession in a stop-start second period. It all looked good when McDonough scored his fifteenth goal of season to give the U's the lead. Roberts picked out McGavin with a free-kick, and the striker made space for himself before crossing from the left. McDonough scored a picture goal with a diving header. Hesitation in the Redbridge defence almost allowed Colchester a second goal two minutes later, but Gary Bennett's first-time shot went over the bar. Cavell fired into the side netting, before the U's felt they should have had a penalty when Mayes brought down Bennett as he went for McGavin's cross. Redbridge's twentieth-minute equaliser certainly left question marks about the lack of marking in the U's defence. After Ebdon's corner had been knocked back out to him, he crossed to the far post, where Pamphlett was left unmarked to head home from close range. After this, the match lost any sort of pattern or rhythm, with referee John Smyth constantly using his whistle and booking four players inside thirteen minutes: Roberts and McDonough for the U's and Redbridge's Walsh and Ebdon. McDonough's seventh booking of the season means that he will now be suspended, starting with the FA Trophy tie against Kingstonian on 11 January. Just before half-time, both sides went close to scoring again. In the fortieth minute, Richardson, who did not

Tony Pamphlett, Redbridge Forest's central defender scores the equaliser in the Boxing Day Essex derby against Colchester United which attracted Forest's highest ever gate of 2,327.

reappear after the interval, burst through the middle and his twenty-yard shot was saved brilliantly by Barrett at full length. Then in injury time, McDonough was only just off-target with a header from McGavin's cross. The second half was a nondescript affair, with the U's huffng and puffing to no great effect, and a draw looked the likely outcome. But with nine minutes remaining, Redbridge broke away down the right with Jacques feeding Cavell. His low cross into the penalty area found the U's lacking in numbers, and an unmarked Walsh fired home. Barrett got a hand to the ball, but was unable to prevent it from going into the net. The closing minutes saw Colchester camped in the Redbridge half, but they were unable to create a worthwhile opportunity and the home side were able to collect the points.

Redbridge: I. Bennett, Jacques, Watts, Pamphlett, Connor, Ebdon, Mayes, Richardson (*sub* Broom 45), Cavell, Walsh, Blackford. *Unused sub:* Davidson.
Colchester: Barrett, Donald, Roberts, Kinsella, English, Elliott, Cook (*sub* Collins 84), G. Bennett (*sub* Restarick 84), McDonough, McGavin, Smith.

COLCHESTER WIN WELL IN THE END

Saturday 28 December 1991
Referee: Mr E.J. Wolstenholme
(Blackburn)

Runcorn 1 Colchester 3
Attendance: 883

By Neal Manning, *East Anglian Daily Times*

Colchester United re-established their seven-point lead at the top of the GM Vauxhall Conference table with their seventh away victory, against Runcorn at Canal Street on Saturday, and, at the same time, topped the fifty-point mark for the season. In the first period of the match, Colchester showed uncharacteristic frailty at the back. They were often caught square, with Roberts failing to drop off in his sweeper's role. Runcorn went at a hesitant defence, which Elliott admitted 'was at sixes and sevens'. With a bit of luck, they could have made the U's task a much more difficult one.

Ran out of steam

After the interval, Colchester sorted themselves out and Runcorn, despite playing down the pronounced slope, ran out of steam and posed few problems, while the visitors stepped up a gear and showed some of their quality in the latter stages. Another goal apiece for McGavin and Bennett means that the two U's strikers have ended up joint leading scorers in the Conference for December, and they will receive the £250 *Mail on Sunday* award. McGavin is now the U's overall leading scorer with sixteen goals, followed by Bennett and McDonough on fifteen apiece. All Bennett's goals have come in the Conference, whereas McDonough's and McGavin's totals include both league and cup matches.

Square defence

United, who have been early scorers in recent matches, found themselves trailing in the eighth minute, as Runcorn took advantage of a square defence. Brabin's through-ball found Saunders and, with Roberts failing to put in the necessary challenge, the Runcorn striker went on to steer his shot wide of Barrett and into the corner of the net. Roberts accepted the blame for the goal. At this stage, the U's looked vulnerable every time Runcorn attacked and, after a quarter-of-an-hour, they had an escape when McCarty broke through. After his shot beat the advancing Barrett, the ball came back off the foot of the post. Within a minute, against the run of play, Colchester equalised with a fine strike from Bennett as he volleyed a McGavin cross into the roof of the net, after Donald and McGavin had carved out an opening on the right.

Unexpected boost

Even this unexpected boost did nothing to shake the U's out of their defensive lethargy. The midfield, in which Collins returned in place of Kinsella, failed to get to grips with a wave of Runcorn attacks. But it was United who came close to taking the lead in the thirty-sixth minute, when Cook hit the bar with a well-struck shot from the edge of the

Runcorn's Daryl McCarty, having broken through, slips the ball past Scott Barrett, the Colchester 'keeper, only to see his shot rebound off the post.

penalty area, after McDonough had laid Smith's cross neatly back into his path. After a rather scrappy opening to the second half, the U's came into their own and took a grip on the match as Runcorn began to tire. From the time McGavin missed a good opportunity in the sixty-fifth minute, when he shot against Williams' legs, Colchester took charge. Four minutes later, they scored the vital second goal. It was Cook's second since he came on loan from Southend in October. Collins, inside his own half, knocked the ball up to McDonough, who then swept it out to the left, where Hughes committed himself and allowed Smith to go past him. His cross picked out Cook in an unmarked position, and his firm header from at least ten yards out flew into the top corner of the net.

Important save

Bennett's intended cross in the seventy-ninth minute went over Williams and grazed the bar before McGavin squandered another fine chance, firing over the top after making room for himself with his left foot. Barrett was called upon to make an important eighty-eighth-minute save from Shaughnessy in a rare Runcorn attack, before McGavin broke way to score a fine solo goal in the first minute of injury time. Donald pumped the ball forward and McGavin, showing good close control, held off Bates before tucking the ball into the bottom corner of the net. It was a fitting finish to send the U's large travelling support home happy and into the New Year full of hope.

Runcorn: Williams, Bates, Mullen, Redman, Hill, Hughes (*sub* Richards 76), Brabin, Withers, Shaughnessy, Saunders, McCarty. *Unused sub:* Waring.
Colchester: Barrett, Donald, Roberts, Cook (*sub* Kinsella 76), English, Elliott, Collins, Bennett, McDonough, McGavin, Smith. *Unused sub:* Restarick.

McGAVIN KEEPS U'S SEVEN UP

Wednesday 1 January 1992
Referee: Mr K. Bullivant (Cambridge)

Colchester 1 Redbridge Forest 0
Attendance: 4,773

By Neal Manning, *East Anglian Daily Times*

Steve McGavin's seventeenth goal of the season gave Colchester United a winning start to the New Year at Layer Road yesterday morning, and at the same time avenged their defeat by Redbridge Forest on Boxing Day. 'It was not as convincing as we would have liked,' admitted U's player-coach Roy McDonough, while his opposite number John Still said: 'It was a fair result. We defended well, but we didn't pose them any threat going forward.' On the plus side, Colchester kept a clean sheet for the eleventh time this season in Conference matches, and the attendance of 4,773 took the average at Layer Road to date to over 3,000.

Encouraging signs

Encouraging indeed, but it would have been nice if a good holiday crowd had seen Colchester being more ruthless. Had their finishing been better, the outcome would have been beyond doubt midway through the second half. The defence had a solid look about it, with Elliott again outstanding. They restricted Redbridge to just one clearcut opportunity, ironically seconds before McGavin's seventeenth-minute strike, which was ultimately to prove the winner. A mistake by Bennett allowed Watts to get free on the left, and from his cross, Colchester old boy Walsh sent in a header that produced a fine save from Barrett, diving full stretch to his right to make a one-handed stop. The goal that mattered resulted from a free-kick, awarded against Richardson for fouling Cook just outside the penalty area. Collins' quick thinking caught the Redbridge defence on the hop as he played the ball wide to Smith.

Good work

Man of the Match Smith, who did so much good work both in defence and attack down the left, crossed into the goalmouth where McGavin headed home from close range. Ten minutes later and McGavin should have scored again, firing straight at the 'keeper from point-blank range, after Collins and English had combined from Roberts' long throw to set up the U's striker. It was an opportunity McGavin would normally have put away without any trouble, but it looked as though Collins may have got slightly in his way. The U's were adamant that they should have had a penalty in the first minute of the second half. Roberts' long throw from the left was back-headed by Connor and fell to McGavin, whose close-range shot looked to have been handled by a defender. There was a moment of anxiety four minutes later when Mayes made a strong run down the left before crossing to the near post. Broom just got in front of English to make contact and the ball flew across the face of goal and wide of the far upright.

COLCHESTER v. REDBRIDGE FOREST

Left: Steve McGavin contorts to give Colchester United a 1-0 revenge victory over neighbours Redbridge Forest at Layer Road. The win puts United seven points clear at the top of the GM Vauxhall Conference. *Right:* Despite Gary Bennett's presence, Redbridge 'keeper Ian Bennett stops this Steve McGavin effort.

Dominated

After that, it was the U's who dominated the play without making any more of their superiority. McGavin tried to beat Ian Bennett at his near post, following a deep cross from Smith, instead of heading the ball back across the face of goal, before a surging run by Gary Bennett ended with his namesake making a fine save. McDonough might have done better with a sixty-seventh-minute header from Smith's cross at the near post, before U's made a double substitution, sending on Kinsella and Restarick for Cook and Bennett. The young Redbridge 'keeper did well to block a shot from McGavin which caught a nasty deflection, but a second goal, which would have taken all the pressure off, would not come. Six minutes from time, Ian Bennett made a fine save from Restarick, pushing his close-range header over the bar after McDonough had flicked on Smith's inswinging corner. It was not the most inspiring of wins, but it kept the U's seven points ahead of Wycombe, who won against Slough.

Colchester: S. Barrett, Donald, Roberts, Cook (*sub* Kinsella 68), English, Elliott, Collins, G. Bennett (*sub* Restarick 68), McDonough, McGavin, Smith.
Redbridge Forest: I. Bennett, Jacques, Watts, K. Barrett (*sub* Garvey 77), Connor, Broom, Mayes, Richardson, Cavell, Walsh, Blackford. *Unused sub:* Sowerby.

COLCHESTER'S WELSH GRAVEYARD

Saturday 4 January 1992   **Merthyr Tydfil 2 Colchester 0**
Referee: Mr D. Colwell (Kidderminster)   Attendance: 1,032

By Neal Manning, *East Anglian Daily Times*

Pennydarren Park has become a graveyard for Colchester United since they were relegated to the GM Vauxhall Conference. Saturday's 2-0 defeat – their third of the season – means that on their last two visits to South Wales they have conceded five goals and failed to score. Yet they had plenty of chances to put the record straight and should have buried Merthyr Tydfil by the interval. But the U's, the most prolific scorers in the Conference, drew a blank for the first time in twenty-five league matches and went on to suffer their second away defeat in ten days.

Missed opportunity

With rivals Wycombe Wanderers being held to a draw at Bath, Colchester missed the opportunity of opening up a nine-point gap. The U's were made to pay as Merthyr, boosted by an opening fifty-fourth-minute goal, never looked back and could easily have won by a bigger margin by the end. 'We chased the game too early after they had scored,' said a bitterly disappointed Roy McDonough. 'In the first half, we played as well as we have done away from home this season without making it count. Once they scored, it gave them a tremendous lift.' In the second half, in which substitute Grainger and Elliott were booked for fouls, the U's were made to look an ordinary side indeed, as an inspired Merthyr pulled them apart.

Brilliant Barrett

The home side had ten shots on target and were only denied further goals by the brilliance of Barrett, who made a number of crucial saves. The early injury to Cook, who was caught in the face by Coates as he tried an overhead kick, cannot be used as an excuse for this defeat. Cook, who had moved to right-back in the absence of the injured Donald, broke his nose for the fourth time in his career and also had a couple of teeth loosened. The introduction of the naturally left-footed Grainger did not help the balance at the back and, midway through the second half, English switched to right-back with Grainger going to central defence. Elliott, who played despite suffering from a bug, was, in fact, sick during the half-time interval. On a pitch ideal for good football, the U's displayed their talents to the full in the first half, but could not make their superiority count. McGavin was allowed to run amok, but his finishing was way below par. The club's leading scorer, with seventeen goals to date, could so easily have had a hat-trick after working his way into numerous ideal positions, but he never once forced Wager to make a save. The U's came close to taking a third-minute lead when McDonough's header from Collins's cross hit Mark Williams on the shoulder and spooned against the bar, while on the stroke of half-time McDonough was only inches away with another header from Grainger's deep cross.

Shaun Elliott powers in a goalbound header in the recent Essex derby at Layer Road between Colchester United and Redbridge Forest.

Hutchinson effective

In the second half, Merthyr made sure they cut out the service to McGavin and hit Colchester with Coates' first goal since he came on loan from Swansea a month ago. Coates squeezed a header just inside the post, after the lively Ceri Williams had supplied the cross with the U's flatfooted. With the veteran Hutchinson, now forty-four, imposing himself on the match and Ceri Williams threatening every time he had the ball, it was no surprise when Merthyr scored again in the eighty-third minute. Coates played the ball out to Rogers on the left and, from his cross to the near post, D'Auria got in front of Barrett to glide a header into the net. There was still time for the transfer-seeking Barrett to bring off two more fine saves, as cock-a-hoop Merthyr were running rings round the U's, who had been well beaten in the end. It had been the classic game of two halves, with Colchester missing out on both accounts, much to the disappointment of their travelling fans, who had boosted Merthyr's attendance to over 1,000 for only the second time this season.

Merthyr: Wager, M. Williams, James, Doyle (*sub* Tucker 65), Lewis, Rogers, Beattie, Coates, D'Auria, Hutchinson, C. Wllliams. *Unused sub:* Webley.
Colchester: Barrett, Cook (*sub* Grainger 27), Roberts, Kinsella, English, Elliott, Collins, Bennett (*sub* Restarick 50), McDonough, McGavin, Smith.

BARRETT THE HERO IN GREAT ESCAPE BY U'S

Saturday 11 January 1992

Referee: Mr P. Taylor (Cheshunt)

Colchester 2 Kingstonian 2
(FA Trophy first round)
Attendance: 2,724

By Neal Manning, *East Anglian Daily Times*

Scott Barrett has been making a habit of grabbing the headlines this season. A last-minute winner at Wycombe in September; a shock transfer request two days before Christmas and, on Saturday, the decisive part in Colchester United's injury-time equaliser that keeps their Vauxhall FA Trophy hopes alive. There were already ninety-two minutes showing on the clock when the U's goalkeeper decided to desert his normal post, as Smith was preparing to take his side's fifteenth corner. Barrett raced upfield to position himself in the Kingstonian penalty area. Smith's corner was headed out back to him, but when he swung the ball over again from the right, Barrett headed the ball forward and English, who had been pushed up front for the last quarter of an hour, headed home.

Congratulations

Supporters raced on to the pitch – mainly out of sheer relief – to congratulate Barrett. 'I could see by the clock there were only seconds to go and I thought we might as well lose 3-1 as 2-1 if my move backfired. The guy who marked me when the corner first came over decided to leave me when the ball came over a second time. But I can't say that I leapt like a salmon!' said the U's 'keeper. Ironically, it was one of the few times that Colchester, badly missing the height of their suspended player-coach Roy McDonough, had won a ball in the air. But Barrett's assist allowed English to score his first cup goal for the club and earn a replay tomorrow night that they certainly didn't deserve. 'We got out of jail', admitted McDonough, after watching his side give their worst performance for a long, long time. 'We were too nice all round the pitch and didn't win a knockdown for an hour. Now the players owe everybody a good display in the replay', said McDonough, who is hoping that Collins will be fit. The little Irishman went to hospital after the game for an X-ray on a suspected fracture of the right shin, but it turned out to be bad bruising. Kingstonian, of the Diadora Premier League with everything to gain and nothing to lose against the Trophy favourites, were only seconds away from a giant-killing act, but in the end were left to reflect on what might have been. Twice they were denied by the woodwork in the second half, but their manager Chris Kelly said: 'We would have been delighted with this result before the match, but now we are very disappointed. We had enough chances to have wrapped it up before their equaliser.' Cherry, a former U's apprentice, struck the inside of the far post in the seventy-fourth minute and, three minutes before English's goal, hit the bar with a twenty-five-yard effort. From a Colchester point of view, the tie was a nightmare. Insecure at the back, they lacked the necessary bite in midfield to stop Kingstonian coming forward almost at will. The longer the match went on, passes began to go astray and anything put in the air was easily dealt with by the

COLCHESTER v. KINGSTONIAN

Colchester 'keeper Scott Barrett just can't keep out of the news. After scoring the winner at Wycombe with a long punt on a greasy surface earlier in the season (pictured), he joins the U's attack for a late corner sparing Colchester blushes as his headed assist leaves Tony English to level the FA Trophy score to 2-2 against Kingstonian.

visitors' defence. McDonough has his critics, but the absence of his height up front stood out like a sore thumb. He will again be absent for the replay as he completes his suspension, but can now play against Cheltenham next Saturday. Kingstonian, who were positive from the outset, took a fifth-minute lead when Cherry collected a long clearance from Blake and held off a couple of indecisive challenges, before his shot took a sharp deflection and wrong-footed Barrett. Four minutes later, the U's equalised when Restarick headed home from virtually on the line, after Blake had pushed Donald's deflected shot from McGavin's cross into the air towards the far post. But within a minute, Elliott's failure to clear resulted in Kingstonian regaining the lead, with Cutt driving a twenty-five-yard shot, which Barrett could only push into his net – something that will have disappointed the U's 'keeper. But Barrett was to have the last laugh in Roy of the Rovers fashion to help give Colchester a second bite of the cherry.

Colchester: S. Barrett, Donald (*sub* Kinsella 67), Roberts, Cook, English, Elliott, Collins (*sub* Grainger), Bennett, Restarick, McGavin, Smith.
Kingstonian: Blake, K. Barrett, Kempton, Eriemo, Dear, Brathwaite, Harlow, Tutt, Vines, Cherry, Smart (*sub* Davidson 67). *Unused sub*: Pearce.

IMPROVED U'S BOOK SECOND ROUND SPOT

Tuesday 14 January 1992

Referee: Mr P. Taylor (Cheshunt)

Kingstonian 2 Colchester 3
(FA Trophy first round replay)
Attendance: 1,642

By Neal Manning, *East Anglian Daily Times*

Colchester United, lucky to escape with a draw on Saturday in the first round of the Vauxhall FA Trophy, were made to fight all the way before coming through last night's replay against Kingstonian at Kingston Road. Nicky Smith put the U's ahead just before half-time, but the Diadora Premier League side Kingstonian equalised from the first of two penalties early in the second half. Gary Bennett, with his 16th of the season and a third from Steve McGavin -his 18th to date- established a two-goal advantage with just six minutes remaining. But a second penalty for Kingstonian kept the tie in the melting pot right to the end and the U's had a couple of escapes before booking their place in the second round. They next have a worrying trip to Wales to take on bogey side Merthyr Tydfil on February 1.

Bounced back

After Saturday's worst performance of the season, the U's bounced back and showed determination and character against a Kingstonian side who simply never gave up. The bite that was missing in the first game was very much in evidence with Kinsella, back in the side in place of the injured Collins, giving an inspired performance. Kinsella's display certainly rubbed off on his team-mates as the U's were so anxious to make amends for Saturday when Kingstonian deserved to win at Layer Road. McGavin, watched by a scout from Manchester City, worked hard all night and almost gave the U's a first minute lead when he got in a shot which Blake just managed to palm away. In the first half the U's had several good chance to make early inroads into this replay but none of them were as good as the one that fell to Kingstonian in the 21st minute. Kempton's free-kick was flicked on by Cherry and Keith Barrett, left completely unmarked in the penalty area, headed-wide of the far post when he could have picked his spot.

Gift goal

Bennett shot over the top four minutes later and the same player was denied soon afterwards with an effort that was beaten out by Blake. McGavin overran the ball as he burst into the box following tenacious midfield play by both. Kinsella and Cook.

It was, however, something of a gift when Kingstonian allowed Smith to open the scoring in the 39th minute. There seemed little danger when Cook crossed the ball from the right but Blake dropped it as Restarick put in a challenge and it left Smith to finish from ten yards out. He stroked a right foot shot into the unguarded net. The second half was only six minutes old when Kingstonian earned their first corner of the match— and from it they equalised. Kempton swung over the ball from the right and Roberts was spotted pushing Brathwaite. Cherry, a former U's apprentice made no mistake with a powerfully hit spot-kick. Donald was booked

A timely boost. American striker Mike Masters rejoined The U's in time for the vital run-in for both the League and Cup campaigns.

for a foul on Brathwaite before a tremendous 35-yard free-kick from Cook was pushed away by Blake.

Regained the lead

The U's eventually regained their lead in the 72nd minute. After the ball had been blocked mid way inside the Kingstonian half, it broke free to Restarick who raced clear before crossing for Bennett to head easily home. Seven minutes later and the combination of Kinsella and McGavin led to Colchester scoring again. Kinsella won the ball in midfield with a fine tackle before releasing McGavin down the right. McGavin burst past one challenge before cutting in from the right. He appeared to lose control of the ball for a second but regained his composure and then rifled a left foot shot into the roof of the net. Kinsella gave way to Grainger before Kingstonian reduced the arrears in the 84th minute. Roberts handled the ball in the penalty area and Cherry stepped up to crash home the resultant kick. Dart made his first-ever senior appearance in the closing minutes, replacing Restarick, before the U's booked their place in the second round.

Kingstonian: Blake, K. Barrett, Kempton, Eriemo, Dear, Brathwaite, Harlow, Tutt, Vines, Cherry, Smart (*sub*. Pearce 74). *Unused sub*. Davidson.
Colchester: S. Barrett, Donald, Roberts, Kinsella (*sub*. Grainger 82), English, Elliott, Cook, Bennett, Restarick (*sub*. Dart 86), McGavin, Smith.

COLCHESTER WILL NEED PATIENCE

Saturday 18 January 1992
Referee: Mr A.D. Danskin
(Leigh-on-Sea)

Colchester 4 Cheltenham Town 0
Attendance: 2,643

By Neal Manning, *East Anglian Daily Times*

All was well in the end at Layer Road on Saturday, when Colchester United showed top-quality finishing to maintain their six-point advantage over rivals Wycombe Wanderers and, at the same time, take their tally to sixty goals in the GM Vauxhall Conference from twenty-six matches. Their first-half performance against Cheltenham, in which they were denied two blatant penalties, did not suggest that the outcome would be so decisive. But after the break they stepped up their performance by several gears, which culminated in three goals in the last ten minutes.

Twenty for McGavin

Steve McGavin took his total to twenty with two more, but player-coach Roy McDonough, back after suspension to collect another booking as well as his sixteenth goal of the season, admitted: 'It seems at the moment that we need something to spark us off. On Saturday it was a lucky opening goal, but our last two goals were among the best we have scored all season. In the first half, I thought the crowd showed patience and did not get on our backs when we weren't playing too well. Patience will be a key word here between now and the end of the season, when teams will come to try and stop us playing.' The breakthrough that the U's needed came just forty-five seconds after the start of the second half, and, once again, that man Barrett was involved. His long clearance bounced inside the penalty area, where two defenders and the goalkeeper got in each other's way as Bennett challenged.

Empty net

The ball went off Bennett's knee over Livingstone's head, and McGavin raced in to steer it into the empty net. Three minutes later, Cheltenham should have equalised when Neil Smith headed Willetts's cross wide at the near post, but after that there was only one team in it. Livingstone excelled himself with several fine saves before the U's, with Masters replacing Bennett in the seventy-second minute for his first taste of action since his international clearance came through, found their goal touch in the closing stages. McDonough headed home Nicky Smith's free-kick, following the sixth booking of the match – five of them to Cheltenham – and this sparked off an exciting finale, with McGavin and Kinsella scoring copybook goals. McGavin's second, and the U's third, goal in the eighty-sixth minute was a bit special, but Kinsella must take at least the equal part of the credit. Bursting forward from midfield, the young Irishman spotted that McGavin had made a great run through the heart of the home defence. The pass into McGavin's path was inch-perfect, and the striker raced clear to finish in the way that has become the

Mark Kinsella, Colchester United's promising young Dubliner.

hallmark of his game. It was appropriate that Kinsella still had time to complete the scoring against a now tiring Cheltenham side, who had played above themselves in the first half. Receiving a through-ball from McDonough, Kinsella skipped past three challenges as he worked his way into the penalty area before shooting past Livingstone. It was the U's biggest League win since they beat Yeovil by a similar margin in mid-September, and a big boost to take them into Friday's televised match at Kettering.

Colchester: Barrett, Donald, Roberts, Kinsella, English, Elliott (*sub* Grainger 84), Cook, Bennett (*sub* Masters 72), McDonough, McGavin, Nicky Smith.
Cheltenham: Livingstone, Masefield, Willetts, Neil Smith, Vircavs, Howells, Brooks (*sub* Turnbull 81), Owen, Evans, Buckland (*sub* Perrett 64), Purdie.

U'S FAIL TO MAKE SUPERIORITY COUNT

Friday 24 January 1992
Referee: Mr D. Shadwell
      (Bromsgrove)

Kettering Town 2 Colchester 2
Attendance: 4,100

By Neal Manning, *East Anglian Daily Times*

Two goals up in the first eleven minutes at Rockingham Road last night, Colchester United looked to be skating to victory against Kettering on a rock-hard surface, which raised the question as to whether the match should have gone ahead. So much in command, the U's seemed set for an emphatic victory until Kettering shocked them with two goals in a five-minute spell to square the match by the twentieth minute. It was exciting stuff for the frozen fans, and for the watching *Sportscast* audience, but in the end the U's did not get the reward their play deserved. Colchester were so much better than their opponents. They spent almost the entire second half camped in the Kettering half, but failed to score from numerous opportunities. Conditions became worse as the match went on, and the players were often finding difficulty in keeping their feet. The U's, positive from the outset, drew first blood in the fifth minute with McGavin's twenty-first goal of the season, scored on his twenty-fourth birthday. There was no apparent danger when Huxford attempted a back-pass, but the ball fell short and McGavin nipped in, rounded the advancing goalkeeper and slipped it into the empty net. There was more joy for the U's large travelling support when Smith scored his fifth of the season in the eleventh minute. Bennett did the spadework, working his way into the penalty area before crossing the ball low across goal. Shoemake got a hand to the ball, but was only able to palm it as far as Smith, who gratefully accepted the chance from inside the six-yard box. Kettering reduced the arrears four minutes later, with a spectacular goal from Hill. Price's free-kick was headed out by Roberts, but only as far as Hill, who let go with a ferocious twenty-yard shot. Barrett did well to get a hand to it, but the pace of the ball took it into the roof of the net. There was a further setback for the U's in the twentieth minute when Kettering equalised from the penalty spot. The referee adjudged that Roberts had handled a harmless cross from Brown. It seemed a harsh decision to say the least, but Hill stepped up to drive the spot-kick low into the corner of the net. Despite these setbacks, Colchester continued to take the match to Kettering. In the twenty-sixth minute, McGavin shot against the inside of the post. Soon afterwards, McDonough hesitated when the ball fell to him from Smith's free-kick and, in the end, his effort was blocked. Shoemake made a good save to deny Bennett in the thirty-first minute, and it seemed only a matter of time before the U's would score again. McGavin, who was shadowed by Keast all evening, posed the greatest threat to the home defence, as the U's piled on the pressure after the interval. In the eighty-fifth minute, Elliott ploughed forward to have a shot deflected over the top, before a brilliant run by McGavin left him with only the advancing 'keeper to beat, but he flicked the ball with the outside of his left foot just past the post. Cook went close again after being set up by McGavin, before Kettering broke away and almost

Kettering V Colchester Utd

Friday 24th January

Exclusive Live Coverage

at the  3 4 7

Doors open 7:30 KO 8:00

Bar open throughout the whole game
Admission by this ticket only

WINE **£5** BAR

FRONT ENTRANCE OF HIPPODROME

SPORTSCAST: ▪ **12.00** Sport ▪ desk. **12.05** Racing Preview. **12.30** Horse Racing From Southwell & Uttoxeter. **6.00** Racing Round-up. **7.00** Sportsdesk. **7.30** GM Vauxhall Conference Soccer. Kettering Town v Colchester United. **10.00** Greyhound Racing. ● Call 0800 59 0098 for your nearest Sportscast pub.

Colchester fans were able to watch the frostbound clash at Kettering's Rockingham road ground in comfort on a giant screen at one of the town's nightspots. British Aerospace Sportscast broadcast several GM Vauxhall Conference clashes to subscribing pubs and clubs.

snatched an eighty-eighth-minute winner with their only chance of the half. Graham burst clear from the halfway line with Cook in pursuit. As Barrett advanced, Graham pulled his shot wide of the far post.

Kettering: Shoemake, Huxford (*sub* Graham 70), Jones, Nicol, Price (*sub* Bancroft 32), Slack, Keast, Brown, Christie, Culpin, Hill.

Colchester: Barrett, Donald, Roberts, Kinsella, English, Elliott, Cook, Bennett (*sub* Masters 77), McDonough, McGavin, Smith. *Unused sub:* Grainger.

NO GOALS IN WALES, BUT COLCHESTER LIVE TO FIGHT AGAIN

Sunday 2 February 1992

Referee: Mr D. Gallagher (Banbury)

Merthyr Tydfil 0 Colchester 0
(FA Trophy Second Round)
Attendance: 1,211

From the *East Anglian Daily Times*

Colchester United must try again at Layer Road tomorrow night to see if they can book their place in the third round of the Vauxhall FA Trophy. A goal-less stalemate at Pennydarren Park was a fair reflection of a match in which there were very few chances. The U's failed to create one clearcut opening, while Merthyr only had one good opportunity to settle this second round tie. On their past two visits to South Wales, Colchester have suffered heavy defeats without scoring a goal. The goal drought continued but at least overcame the jinx of defeats by showing the necessary determination and resilience to earn a second chance. Defensively, the U's were sound, but they showed little imagination going forward. They failed to use the width of the pitch and their crosses throughout from either flank were extremely poor. Colchester's lack of punch up front against a Merthyr defence, in which former Welsh international Boyle was outstanding, was summed up by the fact that goalkeeper Wager did not have a save to make throughout.

Scrappy

Overall it was a hard-fought tie with both sides cancelling each out. At times, the play was very scrappy. In the first half, the game was tight indeed, but there were only two half chances – one at each end. The first fell after twenty minutes to Masters, who was in the starting line-up for the first time in preference to Bennett. McGavin crossed from the left, McDonough headed down and Masters hit a first-time shot just wide. Five minutes before the interval, Merthyr went close, with Boyle heading just wide at the far post from Hutchinson's corner. The U's had been put in trouble by McDonough, who had played a cross-field pass well inside the Merthyr half which had put his own side under pressure. Elliott brought down Coates at the edge of the penalty area and from the resultant free-kick Barrett had to stretch to tip Roger's effort over the bar.

Back-headed

D'Auria headed over from a good position two minutes into the second half, after a long throw by James had been back-headed into the danger area by Boyle. The best chance of the match fell to Merthyr in the fifty-third minute. A back-header from Donald went straight to Coates, but with only Barrett to beat, he did not apply the necessary finish and the U's 'keeper was able to save comfortably. Masters was booked for four minutes later for pulling Coates back by his shirt. In the sixty-second minute, Barrett was forced to dive at full length to turn round a header by Ceri Williams, after good work by the veteran

78

Merthyr striker Marc Coates (white shirt) is foiled by Colchester 'keeper Scott Barrett after a mistake by Warren Donald in the sides 0-0 FA Trophy draw on Sunday.

Hutchinson on the left. Bennett replaced Masters in the sixty-seventh minute, before English became the second U's player to be booked for a foul on Ceri Williams. There was one more escape for the U's in the seventy-fourth minute, when Cook blocked a header by Boyle on the line, following Hutchinson's corner from the right. Two minutes from the end, McGavin, who had been kept in check by the Merthyr defence, cut in from the right and, after evading two challenges, was stopped by James as he was lining up a shot. Colchester, however, will be happy to have another crack before their own fans tomorrow night.

Merthyr: Wager, M. Williams, James, Boyle, Lewis, Rogers, Beattie, Coates (*sub* Webley), D'Auria, Hutchinson, C. Williams. *Unused sub:* Tucker.
Colchester: Barrett, Donald, Roberts, Kinsella, English, Elliott, Cook, Masters (*sub* Bennett 67), McDonough, McGavin, Smith. *Unused sub:* Collins.

McDONOUGH'S LATE STRIKE SENDS COLCHESTER THROUGH

Tuesday 4 February 1992

Referee: Mr D. Gallagher (Banbury)

Colchester 1 Merthyr Tydfil 0
(FA Trophy Second Round Replay)
Attendance: 2,746

From the *East Anglian Daily Times*

Roy McDonough popped up with his seventeenth goal of the season, just four minutes from the end of last night's Vauxhall FA. Trophy second round replay at Layer Road, to book Colchester United a place in the next round. They will now be at home to Morecambe, who last night beat Welling 2-l, on 22 February. Just when this second round replay looked to be heading for extra time, McDonough, who had been guilty of a glaring miss just six minutes earlier, came to the rescue on a night when the U's missed countless chances to have wrapped up the tie long before the end. Colchester dominated this match throughout, but were let down by their finishing against a Merthyr side that defended stoutly throughout.

Welcome relief

It had taken the U's 266 minutes to break down the Welsh side in their third meeting within a month, and McDonough's late goal came as a welcome relief to all concerned. After the goal-less draw in South Wales on Sunday, McDonough made two changes bringing the fit-again Collins back into midfield and restoring Bennett to the attack. A total of fourteen corners summed up the U's domination of this tie, but it began to look as though it was just going to be one of those nights when the ball would simply not go in. Colchester could have made their task easier, had Bennett accepted a chance in the seventh minute. Racing onto a pass from McGavin, Bennett only had Wager to beat but he shot straight at the 'keeper. The one moment of real anxiety for the U's came in the twentieth minute when D'Auria let go with a right-foot shot from twenty-five yards, but Barrett, celebrating his 100th appearance for the club, dived at full length to turn the ball round the post.

Heroic defence

The quality of crossing was certainly better than it had been on Sunday, with McDonough making his presence felt in the air, but Colchester could not find a way past the excellent Wager and his heroic defence, in which Boyle and Lewis excelled. In the second half, the U's played with the rain driving into their faces, but it did not prevent them from exerting almost non-stop pressure on the Merthyr defence. Bennett volleyed wide in the forty-eighth minute when he should have done better, before Kinsella ploughed his way through but then failed to get his shot in. Elliott shot over before Wager came to the rescue with a fine fifty-seventh-minute save from Kinsella. Bennett had another chance in the sixty-sixth minute when, following a surging run by Smith, he snatched at his shot to

Merthyr goalkeeper Gary Wager denies Gary Bennett an early opportunity in the FA Trophy replay at Layer Road last night. Wager kept United at bay until the dying moments when player-manager Roy McDonough netted the solitary goal.

continue the U's frustration in front of goal. Wager again did well six minutes later, blocking a fierce shot from Smith before Bennett turned on the edge of the area and shot just over the bar. Merthyr had one chance to embarrass the home side when, in the seventy-ninth minute, Barrett could only get a fingertip to a cross from Coates and the ball fell to substitute Webley, who shot first time and wide. A minute later, McDonough summed up the U's finishing with a glaring miss. Bennett made a good run and then provided a cross to the far post, but McDonough, unmarked, allowed the ball to bounce off his knees. With seconds ticking away, McDonough made amends; Cook, who had replaced Donald at right-back, crossed from the right and McGavin's shot was parried by Wager. The ball came out to McDonough, who drove it left-footed into the roof of the net. The U's are certainly making progress in the FA Trophy the hard way, with replays required in both rounds so far.

Colchester: Barrett, Cook, Roberts, Kinsella, English, Elliott, Collins, Bennett, McDonough, McGavin, Smith. *Unused subs:* Donald, Masters.
Merthyr: Wager, M.Williams, James, Boyle, Lewis, Rogers (*sub* Webley 74), Beattie, Coates, D'Auria (*sub* Tucker 59), Hutchinson, C. Williams.

COLCHESTER BOUNCE BACK

Friday 7 February 1992
Referee: Mr D. Mansfield
(Macclesfield)

Kidderminster Harriers 2 Colchester 2
Attendance: 1,828

By Elvin King, *East Anglian Daily Times*

An inspired second-half fight-back by Colchester gave them a share of the spoils at Kidderminster in last night's GM Vauxhall Conference match. Knocked out of their stride by a controversial fourth-minute goal for the home team, the Conference leaders displayed the character to bounce back in a thrilling contest in front of the *Sportscast* cameras. Paul Davies looked to have handled for the opening goal, which caused a furious protest from the Colchester players when it was allowed to stand. This was added to by a superb effort by Delwyn Humphreys in the twenty-third minute. The evidence of the cameras was that there was no handball, but it was hard to convince the U's of that fact. Colchester had a frustrating opening forty-five minutes, but something must have been said at the interval as they looked a different side with their neat one-touch football often leaving their opponents struggling during the second half. Two goals in a minute brought United level during a purple patch in which they could have scored another couple of goals. Player-coach McDonough kept the side that beat Merthyr 1-0 in the Trophy on Tuesday. New signing Ian Stewart watched from the stands. Also casting a watchful eye over his former side was last season's manager, Ian Atkins. As early as the first minute, Scott Barrett could not hold a shot from Hadley and English had to boot hastily clear. Three minutes later, English headed back to his 'keeper and Barrett came out to collect what looked like a simple ball. Davies jumped to get the first touch and the ball rolled into the net. The Colchester players surrounded the referee, Mr Mansfield, and the linesman but, after a long conversation between the two officials, the goal stood. It seems that they were probably correct.

Humphrey's rocket

With Colchester uncharacteristically shaky at the back, Howell had a free shot from five yards, but he delayed enough for a foot to divert the effort. But in the twenty-third minute, the lively Humphreys cut in from the right and sent a rocket of a shot high across Barrett and into the far corner. The goal came seconds after Bennett had been ruled offside when he burst through alone, looking well on the legal side of the defence. This highlighted the U's dilemma at this stage, and McDonough was booked for dissent after he was penalized for a foul. In the forty-second minute, Bennett put McGavin clean through, and he slipped as he tried to round 'keeper Green. McDonough, with arms raised, chased the referee in despair after the penalty claims had been turned down.

Brilliant save

Seconds after the interval, Colchester's hopes of a recovery would have been killed off altogether if Davies had not been denied by a brilliant save from Barrett, after Roberts had

United's American striker Mike Masters celebrates another goal. At the time, he was hoping to impress enough to be considered for the 1994 USA World Cup squad.

lost possession on the edge of the box. Elliott saw his close-range header blocked on the line, and then Green saved well, diving to his right to a low shot by Kinsella. In the fifty-fifth minute, Colchester came close to going three down when Hadley turned smartly and shot from six yards, but Collins was handily placed on the line to stop the goal. On the hour, United pulled a rather soft goal back when the home defence failed to clear their lines. McGavin miskicked, but the ball rolled invitingly across goal to Bennett, who duly converted his nineteenth goal of the season. He looked suspiciously offside, but the referee was perfectly placed to give the goal. Within seconds, McGavin was fouled just outside the area and up stepped Smith top drive home a twenty-yard free-kick that raced into the top corner. It could have been all over within a further two minutes, firstly when McGavin threaded his way through the defence before firing wildly over, with McDonough and Bennett waiting patiently for a pass. Then McGavin's skill took him to the byline and his cross was side-footed onto the crossbar from three yards out by the lunging Bennett.

Kidderminster: Green, Benton, Joseph, Weir, Gillett, Forsyth, Lilwall (*sub* Wolsey 83), Howell, Hadley, Davies, Humphreys. *Unused sub:* Taylor.
Colchester: Barrett, Cook (*sub* Donald 83), Roberts, Kinsella, English, Elliott, Collins, Bennett (*sub* Masters 77), McDonough, McGavin, Smith.

LIVELY McGAVIN GIVES U'S THAT CHAMPIONSHIP LOOK

Tuesday 11 February 1992
Referee: Mr T. Moore (Norwich)

Colchester 1 Boston United 0
Attendance: 3,229

By **Elvin King,** *East Anglian Daily Times*

Steve McGavin's twenty-second goal of the season put Colchester United 11 points clear at the top of the GM Vauxhall Conference. The U's leading scorer struck in the fifty-second minute with a close-range header to see off a Boston side weakened by injury. Their plight was not helped when front man Micky Nuttell was sent off in the sixty-second minute for his second bookable offence. Colchester, who kept an unchanged side, never really got into their stride, although there is no doubt that they deserved the three points that pulls them further away from second-placed Wycombe Wanderers, who have four games in hand. Former Northern Ireland international, thirty-year-old Ian Stewart, made his U's debut when he came on with nineteen minutes left, but the game was decided by then, with Boston fighting hard but giving little indication that they would ever score. In front of the biggest Layer Road evening home crowd of the season, Colchester found Boston's heavily manned midfield a problem, although the visitors were punchless up front and goalkeeper Scott Barrett had a trouble-free night.

Smart dive

It was not until three minutes from the end that he was called into serious action, diving smartly to his right to deny Gary Jones. Boston, who were without the injured Paul Casey and John McGinlay, had three other players booked and showed they had determination, if limited skills. Andy Moore had to play with a groin strain and he did not return after the break, while virus victim Steve Collins, the regular left-back, was called into action for the final eleven minutes from the substitutes' bench. Setting out to collect their eighth consecutive Conference home victory, the U's soon tested visiting 'keeper John McKenna. McKenna impressed all evening, and he ended his display with a stunning last-minute save from a Gary Bennett header that was delivered from a position just four yards out. As early as the sixth minute, McGavin took advantage of confusion in the visiting defence to get in a clear shot, which McKenna did well to tip over the bar. Nuttell was booked for a foul on Paul Roberts as the game progressed in scrappy fashion, highlighted only when Jason Cook moved in smartly to rob Mick Nesbitt as he was about to shoot.

Limited attacks

Nuttell had a thirty-yard snap-shot which flew just wide, but generally Boston were finishing weakly in their limited attacks – this was typified when Jones, from a good position, fired well wide. McGavin was having some lively runs in attack, and he forced former Ipswich Town professional Chris Swailes into a rash back pass that led to McKenna stretching high to tip the ball away. Martin Hardy was the next to go in the referee's book,

Steve McGavin's 22nd goal of the season in the 1-0 win over Boston put United 11 points clear at the top of the GM Vauxhall Conference.

and, just before the interval, McGavin set up Bennett for a low shot that was well saved. The goal came from a corner, unnecessarily given away by Steve Raffell in the fifty-second minute. The defender was admonished by his own 'keeper to such an extent that the referee intervened before Nicky Smith sent over an inswinging corner to which Roy McDonough got a glancing header. Paul Shirtliff headed off the line, but only as far as McGavin, who stooped to head against the post and then lowered himself a little further to head in the rebound. Six minutes later, Maek Kinsella, who possibly shaded the Man of the Match contribution, did well to create space and then cross from the right, but McDonough's shot flew harmlessly wide. In the sixty-second minute, Roberts was booked for a foul on Nuttell, and before the referee could complete his paperwork, the Boston player threw the ball away and was dismissed for his gamesmanship. Shirtliff was the next to go in the book. It was not a particularly high-powered game, with Colchester, although only one goal ahead, looking highly unlikely to concede. Bennett thought he had added to the score, but McKenna livened up the final minutes with a splendid save.

Colchester: Barrett, Cook, Roberts, Kinsella, English, Elliott, Collins (*sub* Donald 71), Bennett, McDonough (*sub* Stewart 71), McGavin, Smith.

Boston: Kenna, Shirtliff, Raffell, Hardy, Swailes, Moore (*sub* Retalick 45), Nesbitt, Stoutt, Jones, Nuttell, Adams (*sub* Collins 79).

WYCOMBE CLOSE IN AS SAD COLCHESTER CRASH

Saturday 15 February 1992　　　　**Welling United 4 Colchester 1**
Referee: Mr L. Mitchell (West Wickham)　Attendance: 1,837

By Elvin King, *East Anglian Daily Times*

Colchester conceded four goals in the GM Vauxhall Conference for the first time as a willing Welling outfit weakened their grip on the championship. Player-coach Roy McDonough is keeping his fingers crossed that this was just a one-off rank bad display by the table-topping U's, who had their lead reduced with second-placed Wycombe winning at Northwich. McDonough was jeered by a couple of United supporters in a north Essex pub when he went for a drink with his wife, Jackie, on Saturday night. 'I can understand their disappointment, but it was the first time this season that we have turned in a really poor performance. The fans have had value for money all season.'

Two days' rest

'We had seven or eight players off the boil, and I shall be having a serious chat with the squad in the morning to find out why,' said McDonough last night. 'We got what we deserved, which was nothing. The lads were given two days off last week in order to rest, and should have been raring to go. I just hope it is a one-off. The small pitch and strong wind did not help. Welling defended in depth and had plenty of aggression in midfield.' McDonough admitted that he would keep a watchful eye on the goalkeeping situation at Layer Road. Scott Barrett, who has made it known that he would like a transfer, can be faulted for a couple of goals the U's have conceded recently. He looked slow to collect a cross that led to Terry Robbins scoring Welling's third goal into an empty net in the seventy-fifth minute. McDonough added: 'For the first time since Scott arrived at Colchester, there are one or two question marks about his 'keeping.' This was only Colchester's fourth Conference defeat in thirty games – a proud record and one that every other club, including Wycombe, would exchange. Saturday's display deserved criticism but, on the evidence of the first six months of the season, it is something that can be corrected. U's supporters made up at least half of Welling's biggest gate of the season. Crystal Palace manager Steve Coppell and Swindon scout Keith Burkinshaw were watching from the stands, with Steve McGavin – or possibly Mark Kinsella – the subject of their attention. McGavin was given little room to shine, although he showed up as well as most with Shaun Elliott having a sound match at the back. The speedy Robbins was first onto Nigel Ransom's fifth minute through-ball, and he lobbed over the advancing Barrett for the first goal. To their credit, Colchester came back and equalised on ten minutes. Nicky Smith was brought down by Joe Francis, and there was no doubt about the penalty-kick awarded. McDonough aimed high and straight, and Lee Harrison, who was signed on loan from Charlton on Friday, could only watch the ball fly over his right shoulder. Paul Roberts lost his opponent and Ransom was unmarked six yards out to head in a

Welling United's Nigel Ransom heads the hosts second goal in their stunning 4-1 win over league leaders Colchester United.

twenty-fourth-minute free-kick for Welling's second goal. After that, Colchester only manufactured one real chance when McDonough headed back to Gary Bennett, only for his close-range effort to be saved comfortably. Ian Stewart came on for Bennett, as Colchester pushed forward. Tony English, one player dedicated to giving 100 per cent each game, was moved upfield, and both of Welling's last two goals came from breakaways against an unmanned United defence. Both times, Mark Hone broke down the left, with first Robbins (75) and then White (89) finding the net. The U's now have a fortnight's break from Conference football with an FA Trophy game against Morecambe at home on Saturday. By the time they play at Altrincham on 28 February, McDonough will hope his side are in better spirits.

Welling: Harrison, Golley, Robinson, Glover Ransom, Berry, White, Francis, Hone, Robbins, Reynolds. *Unused subs:* Clemmence, Burgess.
Colchester: Barrett, Cook (*sub* Donald 76), Roberts, Kinsella, English, Elliott, Collins, Bennett (*sub* Stewart 70), McDonough, McGavin, Smith.

U'S STAY ON COURSE AS STEWART STRIKES

Saturday 22 February 1992

Referee: Mr P. Vanes (Warley)

Colchester 3 Morecambe 1
(FA Trophy Third Round)
Attendance: 3,206

By Elvin King, *East Anglian Daily Times*

New signing Ian Stewart left Morecambe completely in the dark as Colchester United moved determinedly into the quarter-final of the Vauxhall FA Trophy on Saturday. The Northern Ireland international, making his full U's debut, scored twice before limping off with an Achilles tendon injury, as the lights went out at Layer Road. A power failure in the Shrub End area of Colchester meant there was no light in the dressing room, and the well-beaten HFS Loans League players had to feel around for their clothing before going off to their hotel for a shower. Shaun Elliott was missing because of a virus, while Paul Roberts came off in the twenty-fifth minute with an Achilles problem. McDonough moved to defence, with substitute Mike Masters going into attack. The team was further reshuffled when Stewart went off in the sixty-fifth minute. The U's were not at their vintage best, but they were far better than at Welling seven days earlier, and they remain favourites to win the trophy at Wembley Stadium in May. Stewart, who like Roberts expects to be fit to face Altrincham on Friday, said: 'It was nice to get a couple of goals'. His first goal, in the twelfth minute, looked a well-placed shot, but he admitted: 'It was rather a hit-and-miss effort and I was relieved when it went in. The second goal I was surprised to get, as both their goalkeeper and a defender missed a cross and it came straight at me.' McDonough, who dropped Gary Bennett, was delighted with the third U's goal in the sixty-fifth minute, which showed the reason why the U's are on the verge of a notable double this season. It was McGavin's twenty-third of the campaign. 'It was the best goal we have scored since I have been in charge, with a superb build-up and a splendid finish. I was in two minds whether to take the penalty or give it to Ian Stewart so that he could complete his hat-trick but, in the end, it made no difference and we battled hard to win well,' said McDonough, who won a bet with his chairman for not getting booked in the game. Mark Kinsella moved to sweeper and had a very good match, while Warren Donald, brought back into the side again, also shone and produced a number of defence-piercing long balls that could well have led to further goals. Stewart's first goal came after the former Aldershot man had played McGavin away down the right. When a neat pass came back from the byline, Stewart chipped the ball over the 'keeper and neatly into the net. Eamonn Collins had a clear chance after a defensive mistake, but he shot straight at the 'keeper before Roberts departed, and Morecambe equalised in the twenty-sixth minute. Ian Cain tricked McDonough, but there looked to be little danger when he crossed from the left. However, the ball went high over Barrett and entered the net off the far post.

At fault

Mike Allison, in the visitors' goal, was certainly at fault in the thirty-second minute when

United's new signing from Aldershot, Northern Ireland International Ian Stewart was soon off the mark against Morecambe in the FA Trophy. He notched a pair as United earned a 3-1 win, and is shown flanked by Nicky Smith

Stewart scored again. Collins crossed from the right and Allison failed to intercept. Stewart nodded the ball slowly over the line. In the fifty-seventh minute, Bruce Lavelle handled when challenged by Masters, but McDonough, with a 100 per cent record from the penalty spot, this time fired his kick with his usual power, but high over the top of the goal. McGavin's goal came in the sixty-fifth minute, just after Julian Dart, a YTS player, had come on for his second game for the U's. He was involved in the build-up, but it was a telling pass from Jason Cook that released Kinsella down the right. His cross was perfectly placed over the defence for McGavin to put the ideal seal on the move by heading well out of the reach of the goalkeeper. Collins had another shot saved, and McDonough saw his header stopped on the line in the final minutes, as Colchester completed the match very much in control.

Colchester: Barrett, Donald, Roberts (*sub* Masters 24), Kinsella, English, Cook, Collins, Stewart (*sub* Dart 65), McDonough, McGavin, Smith.
Morecambe: Allison, Tomlinson, Armstrong, Parillon, Dullaghan, Lodge, Brown, Lavelle (*sub* McInerney 58), Coleman (*sub* Holden 78), McMahon, Cain.

U'S ROCK ROBINS TO GO ELEVEN POINTS CLEAR

Friday 28 February 1992
Referee: Mr T. Heilbron
(County Durham)

Altrincham 1 Colchester 2
Attendance: 905

By Neal Manning, *East Anglian Daily Times*

Colchester United gave their Conference title hopes a timely boost with their first away league victory for two months against Altrincham at Moss Lane last night. First-half goals from Steve McGavin, his twenty-fourth of the season, and Roy McDonough's nineteenth of the campaign proved decisive in a generally scrappy match before the *Sportscast* cameras. But the U's, after conceding six goals in their past two away matches, effectively bolted the back door and allowed Altrincham just one real opportunity to prevent them from earning a clean sheet. Colchester's performance in the first half merited them being ahead at the halfway stage, but they sat back for far too long in the second period. However, Altrincham were unable to make the most of the possession they enjoyed. It took the U's a quarter-of-an-hour to make their mark, with McGavin opening the scoring. McDonough played the ball cross-field to the left, where Collins headed it forward for Smith to run onto. Smith's cross went over Wealands' head and McGavin, from virtually on the goal line, headed home. Eight minutes later, however, a mistake by McDonough led to Altrincham's equaliser. He lost possession deep inside his own half, which allowed Edwards to cross from the right, where McKenna, completely unmarked, headed home for his twentieth goal of the season.

Tenth booking

On the half-hour, McDonough collected his tenth booking of the season, moments after the referee had spoken to him. McDonough went up with Wealands to challenge for a cross, and the former Manchester United goalkeeper fell dramatically to the ground and held his head in his hands. It was a clear piece of professionalism, and McDonough was certainly unlucky to receive the yellow card. The U's player-coach had the last laugh, though, when he restored the U's lead in the thirty-fifth minute. Stewart earned a corner after he burst through the middle before having his shot deflected for a corner. From Smith's inswinging kick to the near post, McDonough glanced the ball home with his head, leaving Wealands groping at fresh air. The second half was a bitter disappointment, as the U's allowed Altrincham too much ground, but the home side were unable to make any inroads into a defence in which English and Roberts were solid in the middle and Kinsella hardly put foot wrong behind them. Barrett's only save of the night came in the sixty-first minute, when he dived to his right to hold a free-kick from Daws.

Ian Stewart puts United 1-0 up after just 12 minutes of his debut against Morecambe of the HFS Loans league in the FA Trophy.

Second attempt

McDonough gave way to Masters in the seventy-second minute and, five minutes later, Bennett replaced McGavin to give the U's a new-look strike-force. The U's went close to scoring a third goal in the eighty-first minute, when Masters beat two men on the right before crossing, and Wealands saved Smith's first-time shot at the second attempt. Stewart's cross from the left four minutes later came off the face of the crossbar, while in the last minute, Rudge went close with a diving header as Altrincham tried to save the game. The win means that the U's have now extended their lead at the top of the table to eleven points, leaving Wycombe a great deal of work to do, even though they have games in hand.

Altrincham: Wealands, Edwards (*sub* Worrall 77), Chilton, Wiggins, Reid, Rudge, Shaw, Daws, McDonald (*sub* Kilshaw 65), McKenna, Lee.
Colchester: Barrett, Donald, Roberts, Kinsella, English, Cook, Collins, Stewart, McDonough (*sub* Masters 72), McGavin (*sub* Bennett 77), Smith.

ROBERTS PICKS UP VITAL GOAL

Saturday 2 March 1992
Referee: Mr D.C. Madgwick
      (Aylesbury)

Colchester 2 Gateshead 0
Attendance: 2,897

By Neal Manning, *East Anglian Daily Times*

It was an afternoon of firsts at Layer Road on Saturday, as Colchester United maintained their grip on the GM Vauxhall Conference title. After completing their fourth double of the season against Gateshead, and then learning that Wycombe Wanderers had lost at Yeovil, it meant that the U's had regained their eleven-point advantage at the top of the table. For Paul Roberts and Mike Masters, there was something to shout about as they got their names on the score sheet for the first time, but, these goals apart, there was not a great deal for the crowd to savour. Roy McDonough, who collected his eleventh booking of the season and will now miss the Northwich match on Saturday week, said: 'We entertained well up to Christmas, but now it is results that matter most.'

Patience key word

Patience will be the key word between now and the beginning of May, if teams continue to adopt the tactic of putting at least seven men behind the ball in an attempt to stop the U's playing. Despite some patient build-up, Colchester did not function as they can in the last third of the pitch. Their defensive qualities, however, shone through again and, for the nineteenth time this season, they kept a clean sheet. But it was left to defender Roberts to break the deadlock on the stroke of half-time, with his first goal since he came to the club in September. 'I could not have scored at a better time,' said Roberts, who had never found the net in all his years playing in the Football League. His goal, a firm header from Stewart's corner, was his first for almost seven years. It was back in 1985 that he last scored, in a Freight Rover Cup tie for Brentford at Reading. It was the second minute of injury time before the U's scored again, with substitute Masters collecting his first goal since rejoining the club just before Christmas. The American striker surprised Smith in the Gateshead goal with a low left-foot shot, after being set up by McGavin. With Roberts and Masters registering their first goals of the season, it means that only Donald of the regular senior squad has not scored to date. Three successive victories, including the Trophy success against Morecambe, have regained the momentum at just the right time. This has been achieved without influential defender Elliott. Kinsella, watched by Ipswich Town's assistant manager Charlie Woods, again impressed in the sweeper role, but for next Saturday's Trophy quarter-final tie against Telford, the young Irishman is likely to be restored to midfield to allow Elliott to return to the defence. On Saturday, the midfield did not really function in the way it can, with too many passes going astray and, as a result, the strikers suffered from lack of good service. Unambitious Gateshead, who had won 4-1 at Merthyr only seven days earlier, hardly posed a threat, apart from a few moments at the start of each half.

Paul Roberts just cannot stop describing his first ever Colchester goal in the 2-0 victory over Gateshead. Roy McDonough and Steve McGavin appear less than impressed.

Scare from Barrett

There was one scare for the U's, however, when Barrett allowed a long-range shot from Healey to bounce off his chest with the second half only a few seconds old, but the 'keeper recovered in time to grab the ball, as Cuthbert closed in for the rebound. Midway through the second period, United decided on a double substitution, with Bennett and Masters replacing Stewart and McDonough. Bennett, now having to fight to regain his place, should have made the game safe twelve minutes after his arrival in the seventy-sixth minute. He was put clear after Masters had flicked on a Donald free-kick, but with only Smith to beat, he allowed the 'keeper to drop to his left and save easily. Bennett also had another chance four minutes from time when McGavin set him up, but he miskicked from close range. In the end, it was left to Masters to score the U's seventieth goal of the season to make sure of three more points.

Colchester: Barrett, Donald, Roberts, Kinsella, English, Cook, Collins, Stewart (*sub* Bennett 64), McDonough (*sub* Masters 64), McGavin, N. Smith.

Gateshead: S. Smith, Farrey, Veart (*sub* Butler 75), Forrest, Corner, Halliday, Granycome, Healey, Cuthbert (*sub* Bell 71), Grayson, Lamb.

BRILLIANT U'S TURN ON THE STYLE

Saturday 9 March 1992

Colchester 4 Telford United 0
(FA Trophy Quarter-Final)

Referee: Mr M.E. Pierce (Portsmouth)

Attendance: 3,894

By Neal Manning, *East Anglian Daily Times*

A stunning second-half performance at Layer Road on Saturday saw Colchester United reach the semi-final of the Vauxhall FA Trophy, but they were certainly indebted to their defenders for helping set up what turned out to be an emphatic victory in the end. Telford, after going a goal behind in the nineteenth minute, abandoned the sweeper system in an attempt to get back into this entertaining quarter-final tie. For the last fifteen minutes of the first half, they were virtually camped in and around the U's penalty area and can consider themselves unlucky to have been behind at the half-way stage. 'The back lads kept us in it', admitted player-coach Roy McDonough, after Steve McGavin had scored his twenty-fifth goal of the season to draw first blood. During the half-time interval, some supporters were already talking about going to Shropshire for a replay, but the second half was only eight minutes old when the U's scored twice more to take them a step nearer Wembley.

Clinical finishing

A further goal midway through the second half left Telford to reflect on what might have been, as Colchester now look forward with eager anticipation to the two-legged semi-final on the first two Saturdays in April. Clinical finishing was the order of the day, as the U's kept a clean sheet for the twentieth time this season, and are now poised to set a new club record. The previous best was in the 1973/74 season, when they won promotion to the Third Division with twenty-one clean sheets to their credit. McDonough, who is never afraid to make changes, was vindicated in his decision to leave out the experienced Collins and Stewart, who both came on as substitutes in the seventy-second minute when the job had been done. When McGavin put the U's ahead, finishing off what has become a lethal set piece involving Roberts and McDonough, it was just the breakthrough they needed in this passionate tie. McDonough flicked on Roberts' long throw from the right, and McGavin pounced to glance a header wide of Acton, just inside the far post. Telford rolled up their sleeves after this setback and, when Barrett made a blinding one-handed save from Nelson's downward header in the thirty-seventh minute, it proved a crucial factor. Two minutes before the interval, Nelson, who was getting forward well down the left, raced onto a Ferguson through-ball but fired over the top from point-blank range with only Barrett to beat. The tie was settled, however, within the space of three minutes, when Kinsella and Bennett struck. Again, it was the long-throw routine that worked to perfection in the fiftieth minute. McDonough flicked Roberts's throw on, before Kinsella, on the edge of the penalty area, waited for the ball to drop and then hit an unstoppable right-foot shot into the top corner of the net. Three minutes later, McGavin was brought

COLCHESTER v. TELFORD UNITED

Steve McGavin falls to the ground after heading home Colchester's opening goal against Telford United in the quarter-final of the FA Trophy, beating the outstretched hand of the visitors' 'keeper Darren Acton.

down just outside the penalty area. Smith swung the free-kick over to the far post, where McGavin was allowed to head the ball back across goal, and Bennett applied the finishing touch with his head for his eighteenth goal of the season. The final goal came in the sixty-seventh minute, after the U's had toyed with the Telford defence. The chance looked to have escaped when McDonough slipped as he attempted to cross from the byline. McGavin, however, picked up the pieces, found Kinsella inside the penalty area and the outstanding young Irishman in turn played the ball to Smith, who finished with a precise left-foot shot. It was his seventh goal of the season, a sharp contrast to last season when he failed to score. Barrett's brilliant eighty-third-minute save from Grainger's header put the seal on a U's performance that really took off in an unforgettable second half.

Colchester: Barrett, Donald, Roberts, Kinsella (*sub* Collins 72), English, Elliott, Cook, Bennett, McDonough (*sub* Stewart 72), McGavin, Smith.
Telford: Acton, Humphreys, Nelson, Dyson, Brindley, Whittington (*sub* Clarke 63), Myers, Ferguson, Benbow, Langford, Grainger. *Unused sub:* Withe.

NICKY SMITH'S STUNNING WINNER

Saturday 16 March 1992   Colchester 1 Northwich Victoria 0
Referee: Mr M.A. Hair (Peterborough)   Attendance: 3,218

By Neal Manning, *East Anglian Daily Times*

Colchester United and their supporters were certainly grateful to Nicky Smith for his quite stunning goal just seven minutes from the end at Layer Road on Saturday to keep their title challenge on the rails. It was beginning to look as though it was going to be one of those days, until Smith struck with a superb left-foot shot that could be worth its weight in gold. Perhaps the signs of a happy ending were in store as the U's escaped six minutes before Smith's goal, when O'Gorman saw his tremendous twenty-yard shot against the wind come back off the underside of the bar. 'Had Northwich scored then, I don't think we would have come back,' said Ian Philips, who was disappointed that Colchester are unable to find a high level of consistency.

U's less effective

Although the strong wind could be used as an excuse, it did not disguise the fact that the U's were not nearly as effective as they were against Telford just seven days earlier. Roy McDonough, forced to sit the match out because of suspension, did not prove to be a good spectator. He was like a jack-in-the-box on his touchline seat as his frustrations boiled over, and he earned a lecture from the referee for protesting about a penalty that was not given. Having guided the U's into the position they are in at the moment, McDonough is anxious that there will be no slip-ups as the season moves into the closing stages.

Two signings

To make sure he has a strong enough squad to cater for the demands of the remaining weeks, McDonough has signed Dave Martin from Southend and Paul Newell from Leyton Orient on loan until the end of the season. Martin, who was Southend's captain earlier this season but suffered a bad injury at Ipswich in September, will be in the squad for tomorrow's rearranged league match at Bath City. A defender or midfield player, Martin played a key part in Southend's promotion campaign last year, while Newell, who has made ten Third Division appearances for Orient this season, provides goalkeeping cover for Barrett.

Equalled club record

In all the euphoria over Smith's eighth goal of the season, it must not be forgotten that the U's equalled a club record with their twenty-first clean sheet to date. This was the third match in succession in which United have not conceded a goal – a crucial factor that should go a long way to helping them regain their place in the Football League. As far as Saturday's match is concerned, the first half is best forgotten, with referee Hair not helping matters with a series of baffling decisions. When Mr Hair and his linesmen failed to spot

Nicky Smith's crucial 83rd minute strike gives Colchester United another three vital points in the quest for the GM Vauxhall Conference title and a return to the Football League.

that McGavin had been brought down at least a yard inside the penalty area two minutes into the second half, the crowd were baying. It was a decision that could have proved crucial, as the U's dominated the second period, but failed to take their chances. Pushing men forward in great numbers, the home side were caught on the break when O'Gorman struck the woodwork before Smith's winner.

Berryman never moved
Donald hoisted the ball forward, and Masters headed into the path of Smith, whose left-foot shot zipped into the bottom corner of the net before Berryman could move a muscle. Masters headed a Roberts long throw against the bar two minutes before the end of a generally disappointing match, in which Kinsella was booked for a thirty-first-minute foul on McIlroy, the former Northern Ireland international, who showed his age in midfield, as Northwich desperately tried to hang on after the interval.

Colchester: Barrett, Donald, Roberts, Kinsella, English, Elliott, Cook (*sub* Collins 73), Bennett (*sub* Stewart 73), Masters, McGavin, Smith.
Northwich: Berryman, Locke, Blundell, Jones, Hancock, Vaughan, McIlroy, Butler, Hemmings, O'Connor, O'Gorman. *Unused subs:* Lenton, Blain.

COLCHESTER FALTER AT TWERTON PARK

Tuesday 24 March 1992   **Bath City 0 Colchester 0**
Referee: Mr B. Priest (Birmingham)   Attendance: 1,101

By **Neal Manning,** *East Anglian Daily Times*

If last night's drab affair at Twerton Park had been a boxing match, Colchester United would have won comfortably on points. The U's had at least eighty per cent of the possession, but failed to deliver the knockout punch that would have strengthened their position at the top of the Conference table. The race for the title has taken on extra significance, with Wycombe beating Northwich last night to close the gap to three points with two games in hand. For only the second time this season, United failed to score in a league match, but at the same time, they set a new club record by keeping a clean sheet for the twenty-second time. Chances were few and far between in a match that never got off the ground, and it proved poor entertainment for the expectant supporters of both sides. After all, Bath had won 5-0 away at Welling on Saturday, while the U's came into the game with four successive victories under their belts.

Southend captain

The introduction of Dave Martin in the sixty-fifth minute did promise something better. The Southend captain, on loan for a month, went up front in place of the disappointing McGavin, and at least his presence threatened to help the U's make the breakthrough they needed. With his first touch, seconds after replacing McGavin, Martin knocked on a free-kick from Roberts, and Masters forced Churchward to make a diving save at full length. It was the only moment that either goalkeeper was really tested, such was the powder-puff nature of both attacks in the light of two solid defences. English, the U's captain, making his 300th league appearance, did not put a foot wrong in a defence that comfortably halted anything Bath could produce when going forward. At the other end, the U's too often played into the hands of Bath's sweeper, Banks, and the service from the flanks was poor overall. Stewart, who replaced Bennett (left out of the fourteen-man travelling squad) saw enough of the ball, as the U's built most of their attacks down the left-hand side in the second half, but the final ball was not good enough. There was one anxious moment for the U's early on when, in the eleventh minute, a Banks free-kick beat the offside trap and Barrett was forced to race out of his area and attempt to head clear. The ball hit the oncoming Randall, but Barrett was able to recover and gather it inside the area. An uncharacteristic slip by Banks let in McGavin and, with Masters unmarked in the middle, his low cross was behind the American and Dicks was able to step in and boot clear. Cook earned a sixty-third-minute booking for dissent, while Martin became the second U's player to be shown the yellow card for an eightieth-minute foul on Weston. It was after Martin's arrival that things did begin to happen in the

Latest signing Dave Martin joins up with former Millwall colleague Paul Roberts. Martin's arrival in the centre of defence came just at the right time but denied Shaun Elliott a place in the side.

Bath penalty area, and the new boy went close in the eighty-third minute when he shot just over the bar, after his initial effort had been blocked. This result must be viewed with disappointment, and the U's will certainly have to step up a gear between now and the end of the season, if all their hard work over the past seven months is not to go to waste. Wycombe boss Martin O'Neill was sent off for dissent last night during his side's 2-0 victory at home to Northwich Victoria.

Bath: Churchward, Hedges, Dicks, Crowley, Singleton, Cousins, Banks, Weston, Withey, Randall, Boyle (*sub* Gill 89). *Unused sub:* Brown.
Colchester: Barrett, Donald, Roberts, Kinsella, English, Elliott, Cook, Stewart, Masters, McGavin (*sub* Martin 65), Smith. *Unused sub:* Collins.

RIGHT RESULT FOR COLCHESTER

Saturday 28 March 1992
Referee: Mr P. Taylor (Cheshunt)

Colchester 3 Kidderminster Harriers 0
Attendance: 3,073

By **Neal Manning,** *East Anglian Daily Times*

It has reached that stage of the season when results are all-important, and Colchester United could do no more than come up with the necessary victory at Layer Road. Two goals late in the first half and a third in the second minute of injury time gave United victory, but there was not really a great deal to shout about as far United supporters were concerned. In a match punctuated by stoppages, Kidderminster's sole aim was to try to stop the U's playing by putting five men into midfield.

Killer crosses

These are tactics to which Colchester have now become accustomed at Layer Road, but they still should have worn by a hatful. 'We're failing to deliver the killer crosses,' said Roy McDonough, who celebrated his return from suspension with a hand in the first two goals and never lost a ball in the air until he substituted himself in the seventieth minute. Earlier in the season, most of the U's goals were coming from open play, but more recently they have found set pieces most profitable. The first two goals, in the last five minutes of the first half, came from this area, with the third from open play, helped by a mistake from Kidderminster's goalkeeper Green, who, up to that point, had excelled himself. It's the killer touch that is missing from United's play at the moment. McGavin, despite his twenty-five goals to date this season, is having a lean time at the moment, and his form is of obvious concern to McDonough, especially with the Vauxhall FA Trophy semi-final against Macclesfield just around the corner.

Another clean sheet

Defensively, United are sound and, on Saturday, they collected their twenty-third clean sheet of the season and have not conceded a goal in their last four matches. There was just one scare, when Martin's attempted back pass from just outside his own penalty area in the sixty-sixth minute resulted in Barrett having to push to the ball against his own bar. Martin, playing at the back in the place of the suspended Elliott, will have to see the doctor today about a suspected cracked rib, about which he has no idea when he sustained it. It could, however, leave him doubtful for next Saturday's match. Just for good measure, he has three stitches in a foot wound. After dominating the first half, it was not until the forty-second minute that the breakthrough was achieved. Again, it was the well-worked routine of Roberts' long throw and McDonough's near-post flick, which ended with English supplying the finishing touch with a diving header.

Breathing space

The U's gave themselves more breathing space in the second minute of stoppage time from another set piece, which resulted in Benton putting through his own goal. Stewart's corner

COLCHESTER v. KIDDERMINSTER HARRIERS

Skipper Tony English grabs Colchester United yet another vital goal with a spectacular diving header against Kidderminster Harriers.

from the right was again nodded on by McDonough and Benton, under pressure from McGavin, put the ball into the net. McGavin tried to claim the goal, but referee Paul Taylor confirmed that an own goal would be officially recorded. Ironically, both goals came when Kidderminster's captain Weir was off the field having stitches inserted in a cut above the right eye, suffered in a clash with McDonough. The second half was a rank disappointment. The crowd almost went to sleep with the lack of activity. McDonough withdrew himself and Roberts, who was suffering from a hamstring injury suffered at Bath in midweek, with Collins and Masters taking their places. The American missed a sitter from Smith's cross nine minutes after his arrival, with the ball bouncing off his knee with the goal at his mercy, while Stewart was also guilty of passing up a couple of good opportunities.

Goal for Stewart
But the former Northern Ireland international made amends in the second minute of injury time with his first league goal since joining the club in February. Running onto a flick from Masters, Stewart cut inside from the right before hitting a low left-foot shot, which Green allowed to squirm from his grasp and roll agonisingly over the line. With Wycombe Wanderers also winning, the Conference title is still wide open and likely to go to the wire.

Colchester: Barrett, Donald, Roberts (*sub* Collins 70), Kinsella, English, Martin, Cook, Stewart, McDonough (*sub* Masters 70), McGavin, Smith.
Kidderminster: Green, Benton, McGrath, Weir, Joseph, Wilcox (*sub* Lilwall 45), MacKenzie (*sub* Howell 70), Grainger, Hanson, Davies, Humphreys.

U'S ON THEIR WAY TO WEMBLEY

Saturday 4 April 1992

Referee: Mr A.W. Ward (London)

Colchester 3 Macclesfield Town 0
(FA Trophy semi-final, first leg)
Attendance: 5,443

By Neal Manning, *East Anglian Daily Times*

Only an extraordinary reversal or a complete disaster can stop Colchester from heading for Wembley on Sunday 10 May for the final of the Vauxhall FA Trophy. They surely did enough at Layer Road on Saturday, establishing the healthy lead they were looking for in the first leg of the semi-final against Macclesfield. On Friday night, they should be able to complete the formalities against the Cheshire side. 'We've got no chance now,' said their manager Peter Wragg, who felt vital decisions went against his team. But even he could not legislate against the open-goal miss by Green in the sixty-seventh minute, which would have brought the score back to 2-1. Had Green scored – as he should have done – the outcome might have been entirely different, but to rub salt into the gaping wound, the U's added a decisive third goal three minutes later. Perhaps a three-goal victory did flatter Colchester, but as player-coach Roy McDonough pointed out: 'It wasn't one of our best displays, but it was a great result. That's what counts at this stage of the season and now we're more than halfway through to the final.' Over the past month, the U's have not functioned as well as they had earlier in the season, but they have still logged an impressive record, keeping a clean sheet over their last six matches while taking their total of goals scored in all competitions for the season to 101. But it had been Macclesfield who had the first clearcut chance in the first minute of the tie. Askey, left completely unmarked inside the penalty area, collected a cross from Johnson, but failed to make the most of the situation and shot tamely at Barrett.

Good fortune

There was a spot of good fortune about the U s opening goal in the twenty-third minute. Martin picked out Stewart with a free-kick and, as the former Northern Ireland international tried to pass to McGavin, the ball hit the referee and rebounded back into his path. Stewart made the most of it, as he strode forward before striking a low left-foot shot that crept just inside the post, past the despairing dive of Farrelly. Two minutes later and the big crowd were really celebrating, as United extended their lead with their 100th goal of the season, appropriately scored by English.

Slight deflection

English and McDonough combined effectively, before the U's captain burst forward and, although his shot caught a slight deflection off Hanlon, it made little difference as the ball flew past the advancing goalkeeper. At this stage, Colchester were sitting pretty and it was difficult to see Macclesfield getting back into the tie. However, three incidents in fifteen minutes of the second half proved decisive. Martin's attempted back pass in the fifty-fifth

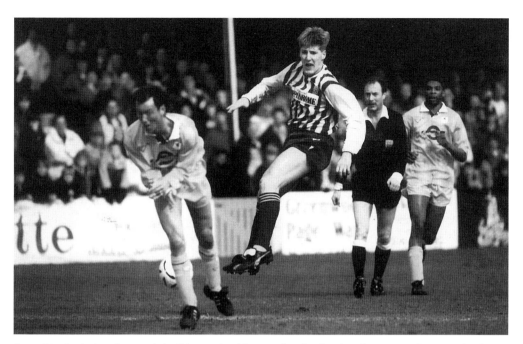

Steve McGavin lets fly as U's build up a healthy 3-0 first leg lead in the FA Trophy semi-final against Macclesfield.

minute fell short, and Askew looked odds on to reduce the arrears. But Barrett, who has played a prominent part in this cup campaign, left his line quickly, spreading himself to make a vital save. Twelve minutes later, Macclesfield again should have scored. Green's miss is sure to haunt him for a long time. English's only mistake in an otherwise commanding display, came when he misjudged Farrelly's long clearance, leaving Askey with a sight of goal. Askey drove the ball low across Barrett and left the unmarked Green on the far post with the simplest of tap-ins. But the Macclesfield player took his eye off the ball and it went under his foot, much to the disbelief of everybody in the ground. The score could have been 2-1, or even 2-2, but the U's took full advantage of their next chance to virtually kill the tie off at 3-0 after seventy minutes. The referee was well placed to see Edwards climb over and then push McDonough to the ground as he jumped for a long throw from Roberts. McDonough blasted home the resultant spot-kick for his twentieth goal of the season. It was a satisfying afternoon indeed, which left Colchester's supporters in no doubt that they will be going to Wembley next month.

Colchester: Barrett, Donald, Roberts, Kinsella, English, Martin, Cook (*sub* Collins 75), Stewart (*sub* Bennett 70), McDonough, McGavin, Smith.
Macclesfield: S. Farrelly, Shepherd, Johnson, Edwards, M. Farrelly, Hanlon, Askey, Green, Lambert, Timmons, Dempsey. *Unused subs:* Clayton, Kendal.

BATTLING DRAW FINISHES THE JOB

Friday 10 April 1992

Macclesfield Town 1 Colchester 1
(FA Trophy semi-final, second leg)
[Colchester win 4-1 on aggregate]

Referee: Mr K.A. Redfern (Whitley Bay)   Attendance: 1,650

Colchester survived a first-half battering at the Moss Rose Ground last night to book their place at Wembley in the Vauxhall FA Trophy final. It was expected to be a formality for the U's protecting a three-goal lead from the first leg, but it nearly all went wrong. Macclesfield, with nothing at all to lose, came out with all guns blazing in an exciting second leg of this semi-final, and Colchester survived by the skin of their teeth. Had United been three or four goals behind in the first thirty-five minutes, they could not have complained as an Askey-inspired Macclesfield at times ripped them apart.

Intentions clear

Macclesfield made their intentions clear as early as the first minute, when Hanlon fired in a shot that landed on top of the net. Five minutes later, Barrett came to the rescue with a tremendous one-handed save to push a shot from Mike Farrelly round the post. It was after Steve Farrelly had been forced to save from his own player (Hanlon) that, from the resultant clearance, Macclesfield went in front and no one could argue about that on the balance of play. Askey, collecting a huge clearance from the goalkeeper, crossed from the left. Green stepped over the ball and, with Barrett stranded at his near post; Timmons had the easiest of opportunities to score. Barrett came to the rescue again in the thirty-second minute as the U's were caught out. Ellis beat Stewart in the tackle to thread the ball through to Askey. Once again, the defensive cover was missing with Green completely unmarked, but Barrett came out quickly and saved at the expense of a corner.

Rolled along line

There was another nasty moment seconds later when Barrett could only push Askey's corner onto the post and the ball rolled agonizingly along the goal line before Smith cleared. English made a vital clearance under pressure from Hanlon in the thirty-eighth minute before the U's popped up with the goal that meant so much to them on the night to relieve the pressure. McDonough's men had survived, rather uncomfortably at times, and then Jason Cook popped up with a tremendous strike to give the Essex side the most timely of boosts.

Cook's third of season

Cook's third goal of the season enabled the U's to restore their three-goal advantage and leave Macclesfield, once again, with a mountain to climb. The referee had added almost five minutes for injury and time-wasting when Cook struck, much to the delight of the large army of fans. After Kinsella's free-kick had gone behind off a defender, Smith swung over the corner from the right. The ball was cleared only as far as Cook on the edge of the

Macclesfield Town v. Colchester

Jason Cook sends 800 travelling U's fans into delirium with a stunning volley. Cook (partially hidden by Macclesfield's Timmons – number 10) ensures that United reach Wembley with a 4-1 aggregate win over Macclesfield Town.

penalty area and he let go with tremendous right-foot shot that hit the back of the net before the goalkeeper could move a muscle. Macclesfield's players looked as though they had been hit by a ten-ton truck while the U's went into the half-time interval certainly grateful for Cook's golden goal. In the second half Colchester were far more composed and took the match to the home side for most of the half. Chances were few and far between as the U's were content to consolidate and push the ball around whenever they could. McDonough gave way to Masters in the seventieth minute and, with his first touch, he laid on a chance for McGavin but Farrelly came to the rescue with a fine save. Bennett replaced McGavin in the seventy-seventh minute, but the rest of this tie was now of academic interest, with the U's very much on their way to Wembley. When the final whistle went, the fans stormed onto the pitch to congratulate their heroes and the players took a salute from the director's box to give the evening a noisy and memorable finale.

Macclesfield: S. Farrelly, Shepherd, Johnson, Edwards, M. Farrelly (*sub* Boughey 33), Hanlon, Askey, Green, Lambert, Timmons, Ellis (*sub* Clayton 62).
Colchester: Barrett, Donald, Roberts, Kinsella, English, Martin, Cook, Stewart, McDonough (*sub* Masters 70), McGavin (*sub* Bennett 77), Smith.

U'S STORM BACK TO THE TOP

Tuesday 14 April 1992
Referee: Mr J.F. Moore (Norwich)

Colchester 4 Slough Town 0
Attendance: 3,197

By Neal Manning, *East Anglian Daily Times*

The GM Vauxhall Conference title is back in the melting pot as Colchester United regained the lead last night by virtue of goal difference. The U's, with the help of three late goals, beat Slough Town in a mud bath at Layer Road last night, while their closest rivals – Wycombe Wanderers – went down 3-1 at Macclesfield. With just six matches each to play, a tremendous finale is in prospect over the next two-and-a-half weeks. Heavy rain that fell for more than two hours before the start left the pitch with plenty of surface water, and conditions got worse as the game progressed.

Dominated

Colchester dominated the match practically from start to finish, but had to wait until the fifty-eighth minute for the breakthrough. Once substitute Mike Masters had scored a brilliant solo goal in the eighty-third minute, the points were in the bag and, just for good measure, Man of the Match Ian Stewart and Mark Kinsella each scored more in the final three minutes. After the euphoria of reaching Wembley in the final of the Vauxhall FA Trophy by defeating Macclesfield on Friday night, the U's were anxious to make no slip-ups as they resumed their League programme. Conditions proved a great leveller and gradually the U's wore down Slough and were worthy winners in the end. Their dominance was reflected in the fact that they had seventeen shots on target while Slough failed to earn a single corner throughout the match. Desperate defending by Slough prevented the U's from taking an early lead when they blocked three shots in quick succession, before McDonough was booked for the twelfth time this season after sliding into Knight, who was also shown the yellow card for retaliation. Good efforts by McGavin and Smith hit the side netting at a time when Colchester were often caught offside. But there was an anxious moment for the U's in the thirty-eighth minute, which should have led to Slough taking the lead. An attempted back pass by Kinsella slowed up in the wet conditions and the ball fell straight to Scott. With only Barrett to beat, he shot wide from ten yards. It was a bad miss and, three minutes later, the U's felt that they should have had a penalty when McGavin went down under a challenge from Knight. The breakthrough was finally achieved in the fifty-eighth minute, with McDonough scoring his twenty-first goal of the season to add to the four he scored at Slough last August. That man Barrett, who has become a master of the unexpected, raced yards out of his area to clear the danger. His clearance fell to Kinsella, who played the ball out to Stewart on the right, and from his inch-perfect cross, McDonough roared in at the far post to plant a firm header into the net. The conditions certainly denied McGavin when he broke clear in the sixty-first minute. He rounded the 'keeper but, from a narrow angle, his shot stuck in the mud on the line and allowed Stacey to

Steve McGavin shrugs off a pair of Macclesfield challenges in the FA Trophy semi-final first leg at Layer Road.

clear. The ball went straight to McDonough, whose point-blank shot was intercepted by Knight.

Double substitution

A double substitution in the sixty-seventh minute saw Masters and Bennett replace McDonough and McGavin, and the big American, trying to stake his claim for a place, did his chances no harm with some fine work in the closing stages. Masters brought the house down in the eighty-third minute when he made a solo break from the half-way line, held off a couple of chances before rifling a right-foot shot into the roof of the net. Four minutes later, Donald set Bennett racing down the right, and from his byline cross, Stewart had the simplest of tap-ins. Just to cap this performance, Kinsella headed in at the far post from Stewart's left-wing cross, right on time. So the excitement really builds. The U's and Wycombe are likely to fight out the destination of the title right to the end.

Colchester: Barrett, Donald, Roberts, Kinsella, English, Martin, Cook, Stewart, McDonough (*sub* Masters 67), McGavin (*sub* Bennett 67), Smith.
Slough: Watkiss, Knight. Pluckrose, Stacey, Anderson, Mallinson, Fielder, McKinnon, Scott, Donnellan, Hickey. *Unused subs:* Whitby, Hemsley.

SUB MASTERS LIFTS COLCHESTER

Saturday 18 April 1992
Referee: Mr C.T. Finch
(Bury St Edmunds)

Colchester 2 Telford United 0
Attendance: 3,964

By Neal Manning, East Anglian Daily Times

Mike Masters, the big American striker, came off the substitutes' bench midway through the second half to give Colchester United the lift they needed to sustain their title challenge at Layer Road on Saturday. On Tuesday, Masters scored one of the best goals seen this season in the 4-0 win over Slough, and when he and Gary Bennett replaced the out-of-sorts Warren Donald and Steve McGavin, things began to happen. It was a boost the U's desperately needed at a time when they wanted some inspiration to break down the Telford defence. Masters has certainly added more aggression to his game recently, and he said: 'I've felt much better since I had two full games when Roy McDonough was suspended last month. My level of fitness improved and it has given me a great deal more confidence.'

Anxious crowd
The near 4,000 crowd were growing anxious after a first-half performance in which the U's struggled to make any headway against the strong breeze and their passing left a lot to be desired. The second half was much better, but the double substitution in the sixty-fourth minute proved the decisive factor. Roy McDonough, who had received such close attention throughout from Dyson, got away from his marker twice to convert pin-point crosses to extend the U's unbeaten record in league and cup games to eleven. Masters had gone close with a rasping twenty-five-yard drive with his first touch of the ball, before the U's produced their best move of the match three minutes after his arrival to make the vital breakthrough. Bennett, now a serious challenger for the right-back spot, received the ball from Kinsella and played it on to Stewart on the right.

McDonough header
Stewart provided the perfect cross and McDonough arrived to power a header into the roof of the net. In the last minute, the U's player-coach took his total to twenty-three for the season – now just two behind McGavin, who has gone seven games without scoring – with a similar goal to his first one. This time it was Bennett, getting forward on the right, who curled back a cross and there was McDonough to head home from close range. With rivals Wycombe Wanderers beating Welling 4-0, Colchester could not afford any slip-ups it they were to maintain their slender advantage at the top. As in the Slough game in midweek, the U's finished much the stronger side and, at this stage of the season, being a full-time side should pay dividends. Before the last twenty minutes, however, it proved tough going for the home side. So much is expected of them, but patience is going to be very much a virtue. McDonough said: 'We found it difficult to get out in the first half

We're on our way to Wembley. The Colchester United squad pose for their official team photo for the forthcoming big day out at the national stadium.

against the wind and on a bumpy pitch.' In the first twenty minutes, Telford had three chances to cause the U's some embarrassment, with Benbow heading over from virtually on the goal line and Barrett making a fine one-handed save at full length from Forsyth. It took thirty-eight minutes for the U's to earn a corner, and forty-one minutes before they had a shot on target to test the teenage Acton. But the young Telford goalkeeper made some fine saves after McDonough's first goal. That breakthrough relaxed the home players and, in the end, they finished worthy winners. So, one down and five to go in a gripping race for a place in the Football League next season.

Colchester: Barrett, Donald (*sub* Bennett 64), Roberts, Kinsella, English, Elliott, Martin, Stewart, McDonough, McGavin (*sub* Masters 64), Smith.

Telford: Acton, Humphreys, Clarke, Dyson, Brindley, Forsyth, Garratt, Ferguson, Benbow, Gilman (*sub* Cooke 60), Alleyne (*sub* Withe 74).

COLCHESTER BANK ON SOLID DEFENCE

Monday 20 April 1992   **Colchester 2 Merthyr Tydfil 0**
Referee: Mr M.A. Hair (Peterborough)   Attendance: 4,148

By Neal Manning, East Anglian Daily Times

Colchester United made it thirteen consecutive home victories to maintain their top-of-the-table position with a two-goal GM Vauxhall Conference success against Merthyr Tydfil at Layer Road yesterday. With rivals Wycombe Wanderers beating Bath by the only goal, the position at the top is unchanged with few matches remaining. The U's thoroughly deserved their latest success, and could even afford the luxury of missing a penalty two minutes from the end. Merthyr, unbeaten in their previous ten matches, had just one chance to rattle the leaders when Webley hit the underside of the bar in the eighth minute – and it proved their only chance of the match.

Smith and Masters score
Overall, the U's were very much in control, and goals from Nicky Smith midway through the first half and another from Mike Masters after the interval were enough to give them three more points. Warren Donald, the only player of the regulars not to have scored this season, was given the opportunity to get his name on the scoresheet, but he telegraphed his spot-kick and Wager dived to his left to save easily. Colchester's home form has been the backbone of their success so far. They have dropped only four points in nineteen games and, with the defence so solid, they have that championship look about them. They have conceded just one goal in their last ten league and cup matches, and the last time that their defences were breached in the league at Layer Road was four months ago.

Far more positive
On Saturday, the U's were sluggish in the first half, but they were far more positive yesterday, and would have ended up more convincing winners, had they taken their chances. Having survived the scare when Webley turned on the edge of the penalty area and saw his shot come down off the underside of the bar, United drew first blood in the twenty-fifth minute. Wager, when challenged by Masters as he went for Roberts free-kick, could only palm the ball out as far as Smith, who looked up before delivering a precision lob with his left foot, and the ball went in just under the bar for his ninth goal of the season. Five minutes later and Mark Williams came to Merthyr's rescue, heading the ball off the line after McGavin's shot had beaten the advancing Wager. Then James made a vital clearance after the ball had spun off the goalkeeper, following his half-save from McDonough's volley.

More breathing space
In the second half, the U's kept up the pressure. Wager saved well from Donald, before Abraham almost put through his own goal from McGavin's cross on the hour. Colchester

Above: Determination on the face of Colchester United player-managerRoy McDonough as he beats a Merthr Tydfil defender to a high ball during United's 2-0 victory at Layer Road. *Left:* Warren Donald, unsung hero and stalwart of United's defence. Given the chance to get his name on the scoresheet for the first time this season contrived to fail from the penalty spot against Merthyr.

gave themselves more breathing space by scoring again in the sixty-fourth minute, much to the delight of the third-largest league crowd of the season. Masters shot past Wager from the edge of the six-yard box, after Martin had headed down a free-kick from Roberts. It was the American's second goal in a week, and he was in the starting line-up because Ian Stewart was ruled out with a hamstring injury that will definitely keep him out of tomorrow's match at Boston and Saturday's game at Macclesfleld. The U's made a double substitution in the seventy-second minute, with Bennett and Elliott replacing McDonough and Cook. It was Elliott's first action for a month. Two minutes from the end, James brought down Kinsella after he had been put through by Masters, which gave Donald his chance of a goal. Player-coach Roy McDonough admitted that it had been decided some weeks ago that if the U's were awarded a penalty in the closing minutes of a match with the game safely in the bag, Donald would take the kick. But his effort was a poor one, so let's hope it does not prove costly if goal difference decides the outcome of the Conference title!

Colchester: Barrett, Donald, Roberts, Kinsella, English, Martin, Cook (*sub* Elliott 72), Masters, McDonough (*sub* Bennett 72), McGavin, Smith.

Merthyr: Wager, M. Williams, James, Boyle, Abraham, Webley, Davey, Tucker, D'Auria, Hutchinson (*sub* Beattie 67), C. Williams. *Unused sub:* Sherwood.

FOUR-GOAL TEA PARTY FOR U'S AT BOSTON

Wednesday 22 April 1992　　　　　　**Boston United 0 Colchester 4**
Referee: Mr A. Streets (Sheffield)　　　Attendance: 2,035

By Neal Manning, East Anglian Daily Times

Colchester United took the GM Vauxhall Conference title race by the scruff of the neck last night with their biggest away victory of the season against Boston United at York Street. Closest rivals Wycombe Wanderers were held to a draw at Kettering, so it means that, with just three games remaining, the U's hold a two-point advantage as well as a significant goal difference. Colchester, definitely fired up for last night's match, won as easily as the score line suggests. They were given the boost of a fourteenth-minute goal from Steve McGavin and added three more in a seventeen-minute spell late in the second half, after Boston had been reduced to ten men when their striker Nuttell had been sent off.

McGavin's twenty-sixth goal

It was very much a team performance from the U's, who had the match in total control from start to finish, with Boston unable to muster even one real effort on target. The U's were positive from the outset and, after English and Cook had fired over the top, they took the lead with McGavin's twenty-sixth goal of the season and his first for eight matches. Donald, popping up in the left-back position, won the ball on the halfway line and then chipped it forward to Masters. The American sent in a low cross, which McKenna was able to get a hand to, but only to palm into the path of McGavin, who scored from close range. There were bookings for Martin for a foul on Nuttell in the twentieth minute and for McGavin ten minutes later for handball before the U's went close to increasing their lead when McKenna saved a close-range header from Martin. Nuttell was shown the red card in the fifty-third minute for an off-the-ball challenge on English, and it was the second time this season that he had been sent off against the U's, having suffered a similar fate in the match at Layer Road in February. Two minutes later, Elliott, who has been dying to get back into the action in the past month, replaced Martin who had been under treatment for a knee injury since Monday. It looked only a matter of time before Colchester would score again and their second goal arrived in the seventieth minute.

Slight deflection

Donald's shot caught a slight deflection off a defender and went behind for a corner. Smith swung the ball over from the right. McKenna, challenged by Masters, could only clear it as far as McDonough, who fired a low shot just inside the near post for his twenty-fourth goal of the season. Bennett replaced McGavin a minute later, before the U's went further ahead in the seventy-fourth minute from the penalty spot. Masters chased onto a clearance from Elliott and made a strong, surging run before being brought down by Raffell in the penalty area. McDonough made no mistake with the resultant kick. More than 500 supporters had made the trip from Essex, and they were in a jubilant mood. Two minutes before the end,

Tony English scores Colchester's second and the club's 100th of the season during the first half of the FA Trophy semi-final first leg against Macclesfield and wheels away to celebrate.

Masters put the icing on what had been a thoroughly good performance. Bennett played the ball through from just inside his own half and McDonough stepped over the ball to allow it to run through to Masters. The American, who has been a revelation in the past week, rounded the goalkeeper before finishing with a crisp right-foot shot that had confidence written all over it. It was Masters' third goal in the last four games and now Colchester will go to Macclesfield, boosted not only by their performance but also by Wycombe's failure to win at Kettering.

Boston: McKenna, Shirtliff, Collins, Hardy, Moore, Raffell, Casey (*sub* Retallick 77), Stoutt, Nuttell, Jones, Adams. *Unused sub:* Toone.

Colchester: Barrett, Donald, Roberts, Kinsella, English, Martin (*sub* Elliott 55), Cook, Masters, McDonough, McGavin (*sub* Bennett 71), Smith.

LEVEL-PEGGING FOR A GRANDSTAND FINISH

Saturday 25 April 1992
Referee: Mr P.M. Roberts (Wirral)

Macclesfield Town 4 Colchester 4
Attendance: 886

By Neal Manning, East Anglian Daily Times

Can Colchester United hold their nerve when it matters most? Certainly, they must put behind them Saturday's mistake-riddled, topsy-turvy, eight-goal match at Macclesfield, in which they first squandered a two-goal lead and then came twice from behind to earn what could prove to be a crucial point. With Wycombe Wanderers grabbing victory with a late goal at Gateshead to put them level on points again, it has set up a grandstand finish in one of the most fascinating championship deciders ever imaginable. 'The wind proved a decisive factor,' said Roy McDonough, who was not too unhappy with the result. 'The lads were very tired, and it showed, as it was our fourth match in a week, but we showed the right character to come back twice to equalise.' In fact, the U's were only denied a late winner, thanks to a tremendous one-handed save by Farrelly from a Kinsella blockbuster. But, on the day, they did not deserve to win when their previously so-secure defence sprung alarming leaks. They had only conceded one goal in their previous eleven matches, but on Saturday the U's looked vulnerable every time Macclesfield attacked, and Barrett, who had previously kept thirty clean sheets, had an afternoon he would sooner forget and must shoulder the blame for two of the goals. The afternoon started with Kendal gifting the U's the lead as he turned the ball past his own goalkeeper in the third minute with McGavin waiting to pounce. In the twenty-second minute, Farrelly, as he was challenged by Masters, could only punch Roberts' long throw as far as Smith, who lobbed the ball into the goalmouth where English applied the finishing touch with his head. In between, United had come close to scoring on a couple of other occasions, but once Macclesfield had reduced the arrears in the twenty-seventh minute (when Barrett failed to deal with an inswinging corner, which resulted in Lambert heading home from close range), the writing was on the wall. Barrett did redeem himself with a fine double save soon afterwards, but from the moment the second half started, the U's were on the rack with Macclesfield scoring twice to give them what at one time looked an unexpected lead. In the forty-seventh minute, Doherty cashed in on a headed clearance by Martin, who raced through the heart of the U's defence before leaving Barrett helpless with a twenty-five-yard shot into the roof of the net. Worse was to follow when Edwards was left totally unmarked to convert a free-kick from Dempsey, which had been awarded after Cook had flattened Doherty and had been booked. On the hour, Colchester equalised with McDonough's twenty-sixth goal of the season and, in doing so, he became joint leading scorer with McGavin. Bennett, who had earlier replaced the limping Masters, swung over a cross from the right; Farrelly was caught in no man's land and McDonough headed the ball over him and into the net. Two minutes later, another mistake by Barrett restored Macclesfield's advantage. The 'keeper was caught off his line as Edwards lobbed the ball into the danger area and Lambert headed over Barrett. It was another bad goal to

Colchester players were not so jubilant on Saturday as they slipped to a 4-4 draw at Macclesfield. The Maccs were determined for revenge for the recent defeat by the U's which had cost them a trip to Wembley. Pictured are the aftermatch dressing room celebrations from that heady night at the beginning of April.

concede. 'Captain Marvel' English came to the rescue in the seventy-sixth minute with his second goal of the match. Smith's corner was flicked across the face of goal by McDonough and English volleyed home at the far post. With a healthy goal difference of plus eleven separating the U's and Wycombe, the next six days will decide the outcome, starting with tomorrow's vital match at Layer Road when Kettering are the visitors. That's followed by Wycombe's all-ticket match at Redbridge Forest on Thursday, before next Saturday's finale.

Macclesfleld: Farrelly, Shepherd, Bimson, Edwards, Kendal, Johnson, Askey, Green, Lambert, Doherty, Dempsey (*sub* Ellis 55). *Unused sub:* Clayton.
Colchester: Barrett, Donald, Roberts, Kinsella, English, Martin, Cook (*sub* Elliott 66), Masters (*sub* Bennett 47), McDonough, McGavin, Smith.

U'S ON BRINK OF WINNING THE TITLE

Tuesday 28 April 1992   **Colchester 3 Kettering Town 1**
Referee: Mr. W.J. Norbury (Harlow).   Attendance: 6,303.

By Neal Manning, East Anglian Daily Times

Record breakers Colchester United are now on the verge of winning promotion back to the Football League following the demolition of Kettering Town at Layer Road last night. The U's chalked up their 15th consecutive home victory – a Conference record – and the gate of 6,303 was also the best in the Conference this season. Now the pressure is on Wycombe Wanderers who are three points behind with two matches left – but the simple fact is that if the U's beat relegated Barrow on Saturday, the title is in the bag.

For U's player coach Roy McDonough it was a personal triumph as his side put behind them the happenings at Macclesfield on Saturday and turned in a thoroughly good all round team performance. McDonough took his tally to 28 for the season with two more goals to become the U's leading scorer.

Four bookings

Steve McGavin, who has been through a barren spell of late, scored his 27th of the campaign as the U's confirmed their superiority against a Kettering side which had lost only one of their previous 14 games. Kettering were completely outgunned from start to finish and had four players booked as they struggled to stay in the match.

After conceding four goals somewhat uncharacteristically as Macclesfield, the U's were as tight as a drum at the back last night and Kettering had to be content with a last minute consolation goal. It was the first goal the U's had conceded in the Conference at Layer Road since December 21.

The heavy rain that had fallen all morning and well into the afternoon had at one stage put this vital match in doubt. Pools of water were on the pitch in mid afternoon and a local referee was called in to have a look at the conditions. If the rain had persisted for much longer, it would have been postponed. With the huge crowd still trying to get into the ground the U's took a firm grip on the outcome and in the 13th minute Bastock, who had an unhappy night, fumbled a back pass from Slack and from the rebound McGavin, from an acute angle, hit the top of the bar.

Decisive blow

Curtis became the first player to be booked in the 25th minute before the U's struck the first decisive blow by taking the lead two minutes later. Following a free kick, Martin pushed the ball through to English who was brought down in full flight by Bastock who was booked for protesting. Up stepped the U's penalty king McDonough but he blasted his kick straight at the keeper but was on hand to collect the rebound and score comfortably.

Colchester maintained their tempo after the interval and after Barker had been booked for a foul on his old Sudbury team mate McGavin, and Martin quickly followed for bringing

Steve McGavin's sends a header goalwards watched by Kettering's Trevor Slack (left) and goalkeeper Paul Bastock. Over 6,000 packed into Layer Road to see the U's edge ever closer to the GM Vauxhall Conference title.

down Graham, the U's put the result beyond doubt with two more goals in a four minutes.

In the 57th minute, Slack's intended back pass was intercepted by McDonough, whose shot was blocked by Bastock. The ball came out to McGavin who squared it to McDonough and he made no mistake from close range. Four minutes later McGavin dispossessed Keast and cut in before curling a right foot shot beyond Bastock and into the far corner of the net.

Right on time, Kettering substitute North ran through to beat Barrett with a low shot but it was scant consolation for the third placed team who had held Wycombe only six days earlier and by all accounts were unfortunate not to win.

Now Wycombe must win at Redbridge Forest tomorrow night to take the outcome of what has been a fascinating championship race to the very last day of the season.

McDonough, who played such a vital part in last night's success against Kettering, praised his players whom he said gave 'a magnificent display'. 'Whenever we have been under a bit of pressure this season we have responded in exactly the right way. If we roll up our sleeves and produce the goods no one will live with us at this level.'

Colchester: Barrett, Donald, Roberts, Kinsella (*sub* Elliott 72), English, Martin, Cook, Masters (*sub* Bennett 67), McDonough, McGavin, Smith.

Kettering: Bastock, Huxford, Keast, Nicol (*sub* North 45), Slack, Curtis, Graham (*sub* Price 73), Brown, Gavin, Barker, Hill.

CHAMPIONS!

Saturday 2nd May 1992

Referee: G.Poll (Berkhampstead)

Colchester 5 Barrow 0
(GM Vauxhall Conference)
Attendance: 7,193

Mike Masters was like a gunslinger from the old Wild West as he shot down relegated Barrow at Layer Road on Saturday.

The big American, who was simply making up the numbers two months ago, confirmed his remarkable rise to fame with the most perfect sense of timing. Just when the U's needed an early goal to put them on the road towards the Conference title, the 25-year-old New Yorker delivered a stunning strike that would put him in line for any goal of the season award. Brimming with confidence, Masters went on to score a hat-trick to take his total to seven goals in the last six games.

'You won't see any better goal than Mike's first,' enthused U's coach Ian Phillips. 'As soon as that went in the game was all over.'

With two goals to his name in the first quarter of an hour, Masters went on to deservedly collect a hat-trick with another tremendous shot in the 77th minute. How the crowd has taken to Masters in the past month. The cheers rang out loud and long in celebration of his three goals. With the match ball safely tucked away, he can now look forward to trying to take Wembley by storm on Sunday. Any doubts about him being in the Wembley starting line-up have been removed; such is the impact he has made in the promotion run-in. No one at Layer Road on Saturday will ever forget his first goal in the eighth minute. Smith chipped the ball forward, McDonough headed down and Masters unleashed a shot with his right foot on the half volley from all of 25 yards that simply flew into the top corner of the net.

Smith, who had swept the board in the player of the year awards before the match, played a big part in Masters' second goal after quarter of an hour, He swung over a free kick from the right and Masters got just in front of Slater to head the ball powerfully home. The American completed his repertoire with another stunning effort. Donald headed the ball down and Masters let fly with another terrific right foot shot from just outside the penalty area that flew into the corner of the net. With his confidence sky high, Masters adopted a shoot-on-sight policy after his opening goal which had brought the house down. 'I try to stay on an even keel, but even I was ecstatic after my first goal.' Masters undoubtedly took the honours on the day of celebration, but it was a pity that United could not score two more goals which would have given them their century in the Conference. Once Masters had broken deadlock it was plain sailing for the U's who were helped even further when Barrow had Power sent off in the 17th minute for retaliation on Cook.

In between Masters' two first half goals and completing his hat-trick, Smith and McDonough got into the act although not in such spectacular fashion as the American. Smith's tenth of the season arrived two minutes into the second half after he collected a rebound. Bennett who replaced McGavin ruled out with a groin injury he had been carrying for a while, beat the offside trap and raced away down the right. McDonough should have converted his cross, but the ball rebounded off McDonnell for Smith to calmly convert.

Left: Colchester player-manager Roy McDonough and Gary Bennett lead the relentless attack on the Barrow goal as Dave Martin (left) waits to pounce on the loose ball. *Right:* Mike Masters is congratulated by Nicky Smith, Paul Roberts and Shaun Elliott after completing his hat trick against Barrow at Layer Road.

It was fitting that McDonough should get his name on the score sheet, scoring from close range in the 65th minute after finishing off a move set up by Masters and Bennett. McDonnell denied the U's on several other occasions, notably from Martin's close range header in the 76th minute which even drew applause from the referee.

Barrow were limited to just one chance when the score was 3-0 when English made a spectacular goal line clearance from Brady after a misunderstanding between Roberts and Barrett. But United had finished on a high note, although one more goal would have given them their biggest win of the season, beating the five they scored against Bath and Burton Albion (FA Cup), also without reply.

The scenes that followed will forever live in the memory of those who were at Layer Road on Saturday. Let's hope that they can be repeated in the Fourth Division.

Colchester: Barrett, Donald, Roberts, Kinsella (*sub* Elliott 57), English, Martin, Cook, Masters, McDonough (*sub* Stewart 68), Bennett, Smith.

Barrow: McDonnell. Slater, Messenger, Rowlands (*sub* Nolan 68), Knox, Kelly, Atkinson, Skivington, Brady, Power, Doherty (*sub* Rutter 65).

COLCHESTER v. BARROW

Celebrations in the Colchester United dressing room after the team's victory that secured promotion back to the Football League.

		HOME					AWAY					
	P	W	D	L	F	A	W	D	L	F	A	Pts
COLCHESTER UNITED	42	19	1	1	57	11	9	9	3	41	29	94
WYCOMBE WANDERERS	42	18	1	2	49	13	12	3	6	35	22	94
KETTERING TOWN	42	12	6	3	44	23	8	7	6	28	27	73
MERTHYR TYDFIL	42	14	4	3	40	24	4	10	7	19	32	68
FARNBOROUGH TOWN	42	8	7	6	36	27	10	5	6	32	26	66
TELFORD UNITED	42	10	4	7	32	31	9	3	9	30	35	64
REDBRIDGE FOREST	42	12	4	5	42	27	6	5	10	27	29	63
BOSTON UNITED	42	10	4	7	40	35	8	5	8	31	31	63
BATH CITY	42	8	6	7	27	22	8	6	7	27	29	60
WITTON ALBION	42	11	6	4	41	26	5	4	12	22	34	58
NORTHWICH VICTORIA	42	10	4	7	40	25	6	2	13	23	33	54
WELLING UNITED	42	8	6	7	40	38	6	6	9	29	41	54
MACCLESFIELD TOWN	42	7	7	7	25	21	6	6	9	25	29	52
GATESHEAD	42	8	5	8	22	22	4	7	10	27	35	48
YEOVIL TOWN	42	8	6	7	22	21	3	8	10	18	28	47
RUNCORN	42	5	11	5	26	26	6	2	13	24	37	46
STAFFORD RANGERS	42	7	8	6	25	24	3	8	10	16	35	46
ALTRINCHAM	42	5	8	8	33	39	6	4	11	28	43	45
K'MINSTER HARRIERS	42	8	6	7	35	32	4	3	14	21	45	45
SLOUGH TOWN	42	7	3	11	26	39	6	3	12	30	43	45
CHELTENHAM TOWN	42	8	5	8	28	35	2	8	11	28	47	43
BARROW	42	5	8	8	29	23	3	6	12	23	49	38

Top: Colchester fans invade the pitch exuberant at their teams return to the Football League after their 5-0 demolition of relegated Barrow. *Left:* Hat-trick hero Mike Masters shows off the GM Vauxhall Conference Trophy. *Right:* Nicky Smith with the Player of the Year award, presented by Peter Tucker chairman of Colchester United Supporter's Association.

GM Vauxhall Conference 1991/92

Date	Opponent	H/A	Res	Score	Scorers	Att
Aug 17	Macclesfield	H	W	2-0	Bennett 10, McGavin 45	2,233
24	Barrow	A	D	1-1	Kinsella 5	1,480
26	Slough	A	W	4-2	McDonough 4, 24, 28, 41	2,226
31	Bath	H	W	5-0	McGavin 28, 51 Bennett 32, 39, 87	2,416
Sept 7	Witton	A	D	2-2	Collins 27 McDonough 47	1,045
10	Farnborough	H	L	2-3	McGavin 21 Collins 86	2,664
13	Yeovil	H	W	4-0	English 41 McGavin 56 Bennett 51, 90	2,979
21	Cheltenham	A	D	1-1	McDonough 15	1,157
28	Wycombe	A	W	2-1	Smith 49 Barrett 89	5,186
Oct 5	Altrincham	H	D	3-3	Anderson 16og McGavin 35 McDonough 70p	2,653
12	Runcorn	H	W	2-1	Bennett 52 McDonough 86p	2,617
18	Telford	H	W	3-0	McDonough 9, 23p Smith 38	1,109
30	Yeovil	A	W	1-0	McGavin 90	2,365
Nov 2	Stafford	H	W	2-0	Smith 35 McDonough 39	2,139
9	Farnborough	H	W	2-0	Bennett 67 Elliott 80	3,069
23	Welling	H	W	3-1	Bennett 51 Cook 60 English 73	2,933
30	Northwich	A	D	1-1	McDonough 75	1,042
Dec 3	Stafford	A	D	3-3	Bennett 41, 77 McGavin 66	961
7	Wycombe	H	W	3-0	Bennett 33 McGavin 62, 86	5,086
14	Gateshead	A	W	2-0	Bennett 5 McDonough 30	542
21	Witton	H	W	3-2	McGavin 3 Bennett 9 English 79	2,842
26	Redbridge	H	L	1-2	McDonough 3	2,327
28	Runcorn	A	W	3-1	Bennett 15 Cook 69 McGavin 90	863
Jan 1	Redbridge	H	W	1-0	McGavin 17	4,773
4	Merthyr	A	L	0-2		1,032
18	Cheltenham	H	W	4-0	McGavin 46, 86 McDonough 80, Kinsella 90	2,643
24	Kettering	A	D	2-2	McGavin 5 Smith 11	4,100
Feb 7	Kidderminster	A	D	2-2	Bennett 60 Smith 61	1,828
11	Boston	H	W	1-0	McGavin 52	3,229
15	Welling	A	L	1-4	McDonough 10p	1,837
28	Altrincham	A	W	2-1	McGavin 15 McDonough 35	905
Mar 2	Gateshead	H	W	2-0	Roberts 45 Masters 90	2,897
21	Northwich	H	W	1-0	Smith 83	3,218
24	Bath	A	D	0-0		1,101
28	Kidderminster	H	W	3-0	English 42 Benton 45og Stewart 90	3,073
Apr 14	Slough	H	W	4-0	McDonough 38 Masters 83 Stewart 87 Kinsella 90	3,197
18	Telford	H	W	2-0	McDonough 67, 89	3,964
20	Merthyr	H	W	2-0	Smith 25 Masters 64	4,148
22	Boston	A	W	4-0	McGavin 14 McDonough 70, 74p Masters 88	2,305
25	Macclesfield	A	D	4-4	Kendall 3og English 22, 76 McDonough 60	896
28	Kettering	H	W	3-1	McDonough 27, 57 McGavin 61	6,303
May 2	Barrow	H	W	5-0	Masters 8, 15, 77 Smith 47, McDonough 65	7,193

Player columns (rotated headings): Barrett, Donald, Granger, Kinsella, English, Elliott, Collins, Bennett, McDonough, McGavin, Smith, Walsh, Phillips, Abrahams, Goodwin, Gray, Roberts, Cook, Restarick, Masters, Stewart, Martin, Dart (Hazell), Duffett, Partner, Hannigan

	Barrett	Donald	Granger	Kinsella	English	Elliott	Collins	Bennett	McDonough	McGavin	Smith	Walsh	Phillips	Abrahams	Goodwin	Gray	Roberts	Cook	Restarick	Masters	Stewart	Martin	Dart (Hazell)	Duffett	Partner	Hannigan
Appearances	42	38	8	37	37	32	29	31	40	39	42	1	2	3	-	1	35	28	1	7	6	8	-	-	-	-
Substitute	-	-	2	3	6	1	1	3	3	3	8	1	2	3	3	-	1	2	6	7	4	7	-	-	-	-
Goals (+ 3 own goals)	1	-	-	3	6	1	2	16	26	20	8						1	2		7	2					

U'S CLINCH HISTORIC DOUBLE

Sunday 10th May 1992

Keron Barratt (Coventry)

Colchester 3 Witton Albion 1
(FA Trophy Final, Wembley)
Attendence: 27,806

Colchester United brought their outstanding season to a glorious climax by lifting the Vauxhall FA Trophy at Wembley yesterday. The League and Cup double was no more than they deserved in a very physical match in which the U's had Jason Cook sent off and six other players booked. Goals from Mike Masters and Nicky Smith in the first 20 minutes put United well on their way against a Witton Albion side intent on being spoilers. Certainly the Cheshire side took no prisoners, but referee Keren Barratt over-reacted and some of the players shown the yellow card can count themselves unlucky as worse fouls went unpunished.

Celebrations

But Wembley is all about winners and the U's and their huge army of 23,000 supporters were left to celebrate a day which will never be forgotten in the club's history. When Steve McGavin put the icing on the cake with his 28th goal of the season three minutes into injury time, Wembley erupted as Colchester's fans really began their celebrations.

The match was never a classic and was not helped by the numerous stoppages which meant a total of nine minutes was added on by the referee. After the U's had stamped their authority on the final and had established an early two goal lead, a convincing and comfortable victory looked to be on the cards.

Witton, however, reduced the arrears in the 57th minute, at a time when United were least effective, and for the rest of the match they battled away to contain Witton as well as playing the last quarter of an hour with ten men.

The U's defence, in which Martin was particularly outstanding, gave little away at this crucial period of the match. Even with ten men in the closing stages the U's posed more of a threat on the break while Witton were unable to make their extra man count.

Barrett, voted the man of the match, made an important save in the first minute at Thomas' feet after a back pass from Roberts fell short before the U's took the lead four minutes later. It was a goal which had a familiar ring about it with a long throw from Roberts paying handsome dividends. His throw from the left was flicked on by McDonough at the near post and Masters craned his neck to head beyond Mason.

Cock-a-hoop U's twice went close to extending their lead when first Kinsella created space for himself but then shot straight at Mason before McGavin, who posed a threat to the Witton defence every time he had the ball, cut in from the left before curling a shot just wide.

Colchester: Barrett, Donald, Roberts, Kinsella, English, Martin, Cook, Masters, McDonough (*sub* Bennett 64), McGavin, Smith. *Unused sub:* Collins.
Witton: Mason, Halliday, Coathup, McNellis, Jim Connor, Anderson, Thomas, Rose, Alford, Grimshaw (*sub* Joe Connor 66), Lutkevitch (*sub* McCluskie 79).

COLCHESTER *v.* WITTON ALBION

Above: Roberts (3), Barrett (1), English (5), Cook (7) and Nicky Smith look on as Roy McDonough tidies up a Witton attack. Witton scorer Mike Lutkevitch (11) waits for any error. *Below:* Witton keeper Keith Mason collects under pressure from Dave Martin. Striker Mike Masters looks for the loose ball.

COLCHESTER v. WITTON ALBION

Captain Tony English hoists the FA Trophy in front of 25,000 ecstatic Colcestrians.

The second goal in the 20th minute was superbly created and finished with great coolness by Player of the Year Smith. Cook made the opening with an inch perfect pass while Kinsella timed his run down the right to perfection to get behind the Witton defence. He crossed low across the face of the penalty area where McGavin stretched but was unable to get a touch and the ball rolled through to Smith who calmly sidefooted it home. Two minutes later Witton's captain Anderson became the first player to be booked for a foul on Donald.

The U's lead began to look precarious when Witton enjoyed their best spell of the match so far. A double booking in the 39th minute for Coathup and Grimshaw took Witton's tally to three before the U's finished the first half the stronger in a period in which the referee took two more names, McDonough and McGavin. They both can feel somewhat aggrieved, especially McDonough who was clearly fouled in the first place by Jim Connor who then kicked him in the back.

Heartbreak turned to delight for Colchester United player Jason Cook after he was sent off in yesterday's Vauxhall FA Trophy final at Wembley.

He was dismissed for a punch nine minutes from the end but then watched as his team scored another goal to beat Witton Albion 3-1 in a bad tempered match. Cook, 22, had further cause for joy when his team mate, substitute Eamonn Collins, gave away his precious winner s medal to the youngster. A shade unfortunate to be sent on the long walk back to the dressing room, Cook had to watch, heartbroken, while his team mates climbed the famous steps to collect their fully deserved medals. Unused substitute Collins quickly handed over the medal before the players did a lap of honour round the pitch.

Cook had never been sent off before and he explained the incident with Witton substitute, Jim McCluskie. He said: 'The other fellow kicked out at me because I wouldn't give him the ball and my involuntary action was to strike out. I thought I was a little unfortunate as worse things had gone on earlier in the game. It was a great gesture by Eamonn.' He watched the final dramatic minutes from the tunnel entrance after becoming the second East Anglian player to be sent off at Wembley following Michael Henry's dismissal playing for Sudbury Town in the 1989 FA Vase final. Henry was never given a medal, but Cook was much luckier.

U's striker Mike Masters became the first American to score a goal at Wembley and his reaction to the support the people of Colchester gave their team typified the players' feelings. 'It was just incredible to see so much blue and white and so little red and white in the stands,' said the striker whose father and brother travelled from the United States to watch the match. 'When you score it is always an exciting moment but then when I looked up and remembered it was Wembley it was incredible,' he said.

Player coach Roy McDonough had tears in his eyes as he sat in the dressing room surrounded by jubilant scenes. He said: 'These lads have been tremendous and their double-winning exploits will go down in the history of the club.

'When I came off because my old legs were getting tired I knew I could rely on the rest of the team. I thought the referee should have clamped down earlier and he did not have a very good game. 'Jason was sent off for what was really a slap. We scored three good goals to show our skills and they seemed intent on intimidating us but we had enough bighearted players to overcome that.' McDonough collects £50 off team mate Steve McGavin for scoring more goals this season.

McGavin, who was cup-tied and missed Sudbury's Vase final appearance, was delighted by his late goal. He said: 'I was determined to score but when we were reduced to ten men I thought my chance had gone. There was so much space out there that I said to the lads 'give me the ball and I will win the game for you. When the chance came the keeper was over to one side of the goal and it was an easy target to hit.'

Skipper Tony English, the longest serving player having joined the club eight years ago, said he will never forget the day. 'You dream about this sort of thing but the reality was much better. Going up the steps that so many famous players have taken was unbelievable and then to turn round and see a sea of blue and white just capped a marvellous experience.'

Witton manager Peter O'Brien had no complaints and said: 'We lost the game in the first 20 minutes when my players did not do as they were told. We came back quite well but did not do enough against a very good side.

'One or two of my lads have taken it badly but I quite enjoyed the day and tht occasion, and best wishes to Colchester.'

Goalkeeper Scott Barrett was named Man of the Match and reflected in the glory of the moment in the first round tussle with Kingstonian when he came out of goal to lay on a last ditch equaliser. Barrett said: 'It was a great game and it is a moment to savour and now we must look forward to agreeing terms for next season. That is the next hurdle to cross.'

For most of the U's fans yesterday this was an inaugural visit to the Twin Towers — and with painted faces, flags and hats they came determined to enjoy. Colchester United outnumbered the Cheshire fans by at least seven to one.

The A12 was crammed with coaches and cars with scarves fluttering out of windows. The trains were simply packed. The poor people standing on Shenfield station platform, oblivious of the day's football action, were shocked to find a Sunday seat so hard to get. And as for the unsuspecting drivers heading back along the North Circular after a pleasant afternoon at Granny's, well, they were stuck too, in a mass of colour and song. It was no more than Big Roy's followers deserved. A day out on which to pin a great year. Fathers had their children posing for cameras in front of the stadium just as they were hoisted onto shoulders at exciting moments. A lot of women also joined in the fun, alongside smiling grandparents with yet another memory to store, of the day the mighty U's completed the non-league double at the venue of legends – Wembley Stadium.

Colchester's blue and white army cheer on their heroes in the Venue of Legends – Wembley Stadium.

Colchester United's three goalscorers, left to right, Nicky Smith, Mike Masters and 'Silky' Steve McGavin.

Cup Ties 1991/92

						Barrett	Donald	Grainger	Kinsella	English	Elliott	Collins	Bennett	McDonough	McGavin	Smith	Phillips	Abrahams	Goodwin	Gray	Roberts	Cook	Restarick	Masters	Stewart	Martin	Dart (Hazell)	Duffett	Partner	Hannigan
Vauxhall FA Trophy																														
Jan 11	Kingstonian	H	D	2-2	Restarick 9 English 90	2,724	s1	s1	s2				s2																		
	14	Kingstonian	A	W	3-2	Smith 39 Bennett 72 McGavin 79	1,642		s1	s1															s2		s2					
Feb 2	Merthyr	A	D	0-0		1,211							(s)	s1											s1						
	4	Merthyr	H	W	1-0	McDonough 86	2,746	(s)																								
	22	Morecambe	H	W	3-1	Stewart 12 Collins 32 McGavin 65	3,206																	s1		s1	s2	s2				
Mar 9	Telford	H	W	4-0	McGavin 19 Kinsella 50 Bennett 53 Smith 67	3,894			s1				s1			s2										s2					
Apr 4	Macclesfield	H	W	3-0	Stewart 23 English 25 McDonough 70p	5,443							s2	s1										s2		s1					
	10	Macclesfield	A	D	1-1	Cook 45	1,650								s2	s1	s2									s1						
May 10	Witton	W	W	3-1	Masters 5 Smith 19 McGavin 89	27,806							(s)	s1	s1																
FA Cup																														
Oct 26	Burton	H	W	5-0	McDonough 1p McGavin 51, 80p Restarick 85 Kinsella 90	2,147							s2		s1			s1						s2							
Nov 16	Exeter	H	D	0-0		4,965		s1											s1					(s)							
	27	Exeter	A	L	0-0	(lost 2-4 on penalties)	4,066		s1						s2								s1		s2							
Bob Lord Trophy																														
Oct 8	Kettering	H	W	4-0	McGavin 16 Collins 45 Kinsella 74, 84	1,289			s1				s1			s2													s2		
Dec 16	Wycombe	H	L	2-6	Restarick 34 McGavin 86	919									s2							s2	s1								s1
					Appearances		14	12	2	11	14	7	7	8	11	14	13	1	1	2	-	11	13	3	3	3	-	1	1	-	
					Substitute		-	-	4	2	-	2	4	-	-	-	2	-	1	-	-	2	2	1	-	2	-	-	1		
					Goals		-	-	4	2	-	2	2	3	8	3	-	-	-	-	-	1	2	2	2	-	-	-	-	1	